THE ROAD TO CALI

For Miriam,

All best Wishes,

Corinne Chu

THE ROAD TO CALI

A Journey to Adoption

CORINNE CHATEAU

To order additional copies of this book, contact:
Xlibris Corporation
1-888-795-4274
www.Xlibris.com
Orders@Xlibris.com
37145

CONTENTS

For Cali

I didn't know if I could be a mother. I wasn't sure if I even wanted to be a mother. Nothing in my upbringing seemed to support motherhood. And then two miscarriages suggested that perhaps it was not "in the cards." I decided to put baby behind me. But then two things happened. I found myself in a crisis with my career as an actress. What had once been my greatest love, focus, and ambition was now filling me with tremendous conflict. I was tired of having to prove myself. The question kept arising—what am I really offering with my life? At the same time, a series of dreams, chance encounters, and mysterious coincidences began to pull me to the idea of *adoption*.

This is the story of how my husband and I were led to a baby in the far-away Republic of Georgia.

I have based my story upon my personal daily journals, recorded at the time. Though everything I have written is, by definition, through my own eyes, to the best of my ability it is a truthful retelling of the actual events. Some of the characters names have been changed to protect their privacy, or the privacy of others. In a few instances, characters or events have been combined for the sake of clarity and simplicity.

January 9, 1997

After a rainy eight-hour layover in Istanbul, we return to the airport and board a small, cramped plane. Bags are stuffed everywhere, and the seating is so tight that our knees are practically in our mouths.

The language I hear is like nothing I've ever heard before. It sounds like a cross between Scandinavian and Arabic. Are these people Turks? Georgians? Russians? I assume they must be Georgians. The encyclopedia described tall, good-looking people, usually with dark hair, hazel eyes and hooked noses. Some of the passengers seem to fit this description.

We're taking off. I take hold of my husband's hand. He turns from the dark window and offers a comforting smile. We've been warned that because of the economic situation and the severe shortages in Georgia, these planes sometimes run out of fuel; sometimes they have to land without radar; or without runway lights.

From our seat in the back, the engine is thunderously loud and the whole plane seems to vibrate as we head up into the black sky. I hold my breath and squeeze Brian's hand tightly. It feels as if the plane is about to explode.

How is it that I am I doing this? I ask myself. *How is it that I am I traveling 5000 miles from everything I know and risking our lives in this rickety plane?*

I decided not to force a pregnancy. Why have a child at my age when there were so many children who needed homes? I knew I didn't want to adopt close by. I needed to go far away. I needed to reach beyond what was known and familiar.

I'm so glad Brian is with me. He only decided to come at the last moment. He was rehearsing a play, and under a lot of pressure from his director. I said

I would go alone. In fact, I almost liked the idea of going alone—making the decision, braving whatever dangers. I liked the idea of being a heroine.

But then reality hit me—not because of the danger, but because I knew if we were starting a family, we had to do this together.

A Year Earlier, January 1996

Our New York City apartment. I can't sleep. I wake Brian, shaking his arm.

"How would you feel if we didn't have a child?"

"What . . . ?" he says, slowly turning to me but not yet quite able to open his eyes.

"How would you feel if we didn't have a child?"

"Do we have to resolve this now? It's three o'clock in the morning."

"I need to know," I say, sitting up.

"I've told you," he says. "It would be great to have a kid, but I'm okay without it."

"But don't you think you would feel something missing in your life?"

Brian props himself up on his elbow. "All I know is this is putting an enormous strain on you. Why don't we just leave it up to fate? If it happens, it happens, if it doesn't, it doesn't."

"I really hate it when you talk like that," I say.

"Like what?"

"Leaving it up to fate. You have to know what you want."

"I know what I want," he says, pulling me to him.

"No!" I say pushing him away. "I don't want you just going along for the ride. I want you to want it."

Frenchie, our little black poodle-mutt, jumps up on the bed, merrily licks my face, then Brian's, and then slides under the covers between us. Myshkin, our white cockapoo, who is already sleeping at the foot of the bed, yawns and groans.

"Do *you* want a child?" Brian asks me pointedly.

There's a pause. I feel a heavy weight in my chest.

"I don't know . . . that's the problem. One day I do, the next day I don't. I start to think it's too late, not right, something could go wrong again. And

13

then, of course, forget about any acting career. Maybe the miscarriages were a message. Maybe I'm forcing something that is not meant to be."

"That's what I'm saying," Brian says, "leave it to fate." He wipes the tears from my cheek. "I think you should put your focus on your acting. Do what you love." He gives me a peck on the forehead, rolls over, and goes back to sleep.

But do I still love acting? Why can't I answer that question? Why am I feeling so ambivalent about everything?

*   *   *

January 15, 1996

I'm walking across Central Park with Paz, the Mexican woman who's been cleaning our apartment, when suddenly I see my mother. I haven't seen her in over a year, since Brazil. I feel an urge to steer Paz another way before my mother sees me, but I hold myself steady and go forward.

My mother spots me, and I see that familiar look of dread cross her face.

"Hi," I say, trying to appear casual, but aware that everything inside me is locking up.

"I'm just *dead*," she says in her thick Eastern-European accent.

I'm thinking that she looks well. Her cheeks are rosy; her blue eyes shine in the wintry sun. She's wearing a smart-looking white shag coat and a matching hat that softly frames her face.

"I have to rush," she says. "Someone is waiting for me." She looks at Paz, smiles politely and says, "Hello."

I cannot make the introductions.

"Hello," says Paz sweetly.

My mother is always polite with strangers. She asks Paz if she's enjoying the cold weather, if she likes walking in the park, if she does this often. Then her eyes shift from Paz to my feet.

"Those are nice boots," she says. "They look warm."

"Yes," I say.

"Mine are not warm enough," she insists. "I need a new pair of boots. I have to be very careful with my feet. I have a lot of trouble."

I'm wondering what Paz can be thinking. Does she notice a resemblance? She must sense something odd.

"Are you a neighbor?" Paz suddenly asks, almost as if she was responding to my thoughts.

My mother gives a sort of laugh. Then there is a pause, and she says, "No! I . . . am . . . her . . . mother." She repeats, "I . . . am . . . her . . . mother!"

Back at the apartment I take off my boots and peal off several layers of clothing, but still feel weighed down. Why was it so hard for me to introduce her, to say, "This is my mother?" It's been that way for as long as I can remember; there has always been an awkwardness, an embarrassment. I'm ashamed of this. I'm ashamed that after all this time I'm not further along in making peace with her.

I had thought that in going to Brazil there might finally be some sort of reconciliation, some coming together. I had hoped we might finally be able to let go of the past, sort out our differences and meet in our points of likeness—our link in blood. But our link in blood seems to create only distance and distrust.

I stare out my living-room window. It's beginning to snow, but in my mind it's a year ago.

I'm in my grandmother's apartment in Rio de Janeiro, a few days after her death. I'm still recovering from the miscarriage I'd had the week before. My mother is sitting in an iron chair. The large painting of Cossacks galloping through snowy mountains that my grandmother smuggled out of Poland during the War looms behind her. I see from the resentment on my mother's face that she doesn't want me here. She didn't even call to let me know that my grandmother was gone.

"She's dead and buried," she said when I called her. She doesn't ask about my miscarriage. She doesn't even acknowledge it.

"What is there to acknowledge?" she snaps when I bring it up. "It happens to women all the time. Besides, I don't think you're meant to be a mother."

Not meant to be a mother.

*　　*　　*

January 17, 1996

I go see Dr. Cherry, my gynecologist. A vital man in his middle years, with a kind, reassuring face, Dr. Cherry exudes confidence and experience. He's the sort of doctor you can trust.

"Miscarriage is very common at your age," he says, "but I find nothing wrong with you. You're in excellent shape, keep trying, and if it doesn't happen in six months, come back and we will see what we can do."

I smile and feel oddly peppy, but when I leave his office I begin to think to myself, *do I really want to see what he can do?*

* * *

January 21, 1996

Faculty meeting at Jim Lipton's house. He's dean of the Actor's Studio MFA program. The school is getting a lot of attention because of the *Inside the Actors Studio* series that Jim hosts on Bravo. So I'm surprised when Ed, one of the second year teachers, announces that he's not returning to teach this spring. I wonder why, because the teaching posts are so highly sought after.

"I have to have knee surgery," he explains. "But there's another reason. Kate and I are going to adopt a baby."

The news sends a ripple through the room. "From Russia," Ed tells us. "Siberia."

The meeting over, the teachers chitchat over cheese and crackers. I wait my turn to congratulate Ed.

"That's great about the baby," I say.

"Yeah," he says, laughing. "Kate really wants one, and it just wasn't happening."

"Why Russia?" I ask.

"It's the part of the world I come from. I would have liked Armenia, but there were no adoption programs there."

"How old is the baby?"

"Seven months," he says, smiling.

"Have you seen a picture of him?"

"They sent a video. Kate doesn't stop watching it." He continues talking about the baby, explaining all the details. I've never seen him so excited.

"I've thought about adoption myself," I suddenly say. I'm aware that I'm whispering.

"Call my wife," Ed says enthusiastically. "Call Kate."

* * *

January 29, 1996

I had a dream last night that felt so real I'm having a hard time shaking it off. I tell Brian before he leaves for work.

"I'm in an underground place with many different doors. I see my name on several of the doors. I start to open one, but then I think of my father and his dying, and I don't want to go in. I try another door, but it's locked. Finally, I open the third door. Inside, I see a woman with some sort of scarf over her head. She's holding a baby. Her face is covered, but I have the sense that she's looking at me. Suddenly, she extends the baby toward me."

"And?" Brian asks.

"I take it."

"And?"

"I leave that place with the baby."

"Well, that was easy!" Brian says, putting on his jacket.

"Here, don't forget your hat," I say, handing him his wool cap. "Did I tell you that Ed Setrakian and his wife are going to adopt a baby?"

"No fooling," Brian says, opening the door. "Don't forget to pick up the stuff from the cleaners."

"From Russia," I say, poking my head out the door as Brian pushes the button for the elevator. "It was so strange, Brian: when Ed said 'Russia,' I felt this incredible pull inside. Almost a physical pull."

*   *   *

Later at the New School I sit with my students listening to Jessica Lange, this week's guest for *Inside the Actor's Studio*. I'm moved by the way she speaks about her children, how much they've meant to her, how they've helped her as an actress—and kept her sane.

*   *   *

February 8, 1996

I see Ed Setrakian at an audition. Funny, I've known Ed nearly twenty years, and it's the first time I've bumped into him at an audition. He mentions the adoption again. He seems elated.

*   *   *

February 14, 1996, Valentine's Day

We're passing Lincoln Center on our way to the movies. Suddenly, Brian stops in the middle of the sidewalk.

"Let's see what's playing at the Met," he says.

Normally, I'd be thrilled to go to the opera, but we don't have tickets and it's now almost eight.

"We'll be late for the film," I say. "It starts in ten minutes."

"Let's just see," Brian says, walking toward the opera house. There's a huge crowd waiting out front.

"Wait for me," he says, slipping through the maze to go inside.

I look at my watch. Six minutes to eight. *There goes the movie*, I think.

"What's playing?" I say to no one in particular.

"*Turandot*," a voice shouts back.

I've never seen this opera, but I used to listen over and over again to Maria Callas singing some of the arias. I'm suddenly filled with a longing to see it, to know how this *Turandot* resists love and then surrenders.

Brian returns, shaking his head. "Too bad," he says. "It's sold out."

I swallow my irritation. I'm about to run in the direction of the movie, when Brian grabs my arm.

"It's a good thing I came prepared," he says, pulling two tickets from his coat pocket.

The opera is everything I'd hoped it would be. During the second intermission, I spot someone who looks familiar. He's a handsome older man whom I remember I met in Colorado a few years ago. I'd inherited some money from my father, and was thinking about buying a piece of land there.

I remember how upstanding and gallant the man had seemed, showing me pictures of his children and introducing me to his real estate agent. He invited me to join him for dinner. At the end of the evening, he walked me to my hotel, asking with a grin, "Can I come up?" I declined the invitation.

I'm thinking now that it would be awkward to talk to him. The woman standing next to him must be his wife. I want to look the other way, but I surprise myself. I say to Brian, "I know that man. Let's go say hello."

It takes Mr. Scott a moment to register exactly who I am. I detect a flicker of embarrassment, but he seamlessly slides into his polite, ingratiating persona as he introduces his wife, explaining to her how I was looking for property on the mesa.

"This is a wonderful production," Mrs. Scott says. "Zefferelli is so good with this kind of exotic material."

"You're in the theater, aren't you?" Mr. Scott says to me.

"Are you?" Mrs. Scott asks brightly. "Are you in something now?"

"We're between jobs," Brian says.

"Oh, you're an actor, too?"

"When I'm not a headhunter," Brian says, restraining a smile.

"Brian has a side job, placing stock brokers with brokerage firms," I explain.

"You actors are very courageous," Mrs. Scott says. "Did you meet in the theater?"

"Yes," I say. "We met at the Actor's Studio. I saw a piece Brian directed and asked him if he'd direct me in something."

"And she's been directing *me* ever since," says Brian.

We all share a little laugh and joke about the changing dynamics of marriage these days. Mrs. Scott, as it turns out, is a family therapist.

As we chat further about our work, her husband tells us about his recent business trip to Czechoslovakia. The conversation broadens to the ongoing problems in Bosnia, Chechnya, and Russia.

The bell rings for the next act. We start moving back toward our seats, when Brian suddenly says, "We're thinking about possibly adopting a child from Russia."

I look at him, stunned. It is so unlike him to bring something like that up, particularly with people he doesn't know, and particularly because we've barely discussed it ourselves.

"Oh, I know whom you should speak with," Mrs. Scott jumps in enthusiastically. "You must meet Patricia. She's adopted the most beautiful children from Russia!"

Mrs. Scott hands her business card to me as we part. "Here, call me and I'll give you her number."

* * *

February 16, 1996

Call from Lela Heinz, a playwright whose play Brian and I worked on together at the Actors Studio. It was a two-person period piece that Lela had adapted from a short story by Maupassant.

"Would you be willing to do *In the Bedroom* again? It would only be for a short run, but it's a nice theater."

"When?" I ask.

"Beginning next week."

"Next week? What about rehearsal?"

"We'd only have a few days," Lela says. "I'm sorry it's such short notice, but we didn't know if we could get the theater. You know the piece, and you and Brian are terrific in it."

Despite the rush, Brian and I agree to do the play.

* * *

February 23, 1996

The opening night of *In the Bedroom* goes remarkably well, considering we had so little time to prepare. Sometimes not having the time to think too much and just "throwing oneself in" is all that is needed. I love this part. I'm able to explore so many different areas: outrageousness, sexuality, power . . .

But—the next night I come offstage feeling terrible, even though the director and Lela say the performance was even better than the opening.

"I love the anger you brought to your character tonight," Lela says.

Is it the anger I feel uncomfortable with? I had forgotten what this material brings up. It enrages me when Brian plays the count as a comedian, because I feel he's into his own shtick; he's not really *seeing* me—countess, actress, woman, wife.

But I know this is not about Brian as much as the buttons it pushes in me. About being seen. Not being seen. About being wanted, not being wanted.

I stay in the theater for a while after everyone is gone. Only the stage manager is here, cleaning up in the back. Brian is waiting for me with a few friends at a bar down the street. The stage lights are still on. I stand under them letting the warmth fill my body. There is something special, almost spiritual, about being in an empty theater. A memory slips in.

I'm six years old. The light is on me. I sense the light and the "eye" staring at me. I feel a giddiness inside, though I don't let it show. I know to do just what I am told. I know what to do even without being told. My body knows. It's so easy. Move here; move there; tilt my head to the side; smile. Click! *They love it!*

"Great!" *I hear.*

I take another pose. I laugh this time. Click!

"Terrific!" they say. "Another . . . and another . . . and another."
I feel the warmth from the light, I feel my body expanding, I feel myself filling the whole room; I feel I can do anything.
"She's a natural," the man says.

Acting was everything to me at one time. It was what I lived and breathed for. From early childhood, I discovered that acting was the way I could be received. It was the thing I was good at, and the thing people liked me for. It was the way to visibility from a home life where I felt largely invisible.

But what was once my salvation and what I had thought I wanted more than anything, is now filling me with so much angst and ambivalence. *I don't want my sense of worth to be dependent on the outer world's acceptance.*

I keep questioning: what am I really offering with my life?

* * *

March 5, 1996

The producers try to extend the show, but can't—the theatre just isn't available. The last performance goes very well; it's a full house.

Arthur Penn, who is opening a new theater for the Actor's Studio on Theater Row, tells Brian that he would like to use *In the Bedroom* for the first production. He tells Brian that we should look for a companion piece.

* * *

March 8, 1996

I'm sitting over tea in a wood-paneled library with a youthful, "fortyish"-looking blond woman: Mrs. Scott's friend, Patricia.

"I lost my mother very young," she tells me, "so I didn't really have much experience with mothering. I wasn't sure if I could do this. It was really my husband who wanted children. It took a long time to finally decide, but it's the best thing I've ever done."

"How old were the twins when you got them?" I ask.

"Two years old," Patricia says.

"And . . . they were in an orphanage?"

"Yes, but it was a very good orphanage. Russians love children. We found them very affectionate with the kids."

"So you actually went there?"

"Yes, to pick them up."

"I hope you don't mind my asking," I say, "but did you want younger kids? We've been thinking we might want to get an infant, but I heard it's not so easy from Russia."

"I'm not sure," Patricia says. "For myself, I was very glad to bypass the diaper stage. But if you want to get a child under a year old, you should call Terry Johnson in San Francisco; she's the woman we worked with. She's absolutely wonderful."

She takes me into her spacious kitchen to meet her six-year-old twins, a boy and a girl. They're seated at an oak table, having milk and cookies. A Chinese man in a white smock and apron is stirring something in a wok over a large, high-tech stove. The little girl looks up, friendly and eager to please, but her brother seems a bit shy. They're beautiful kids, with blond hair, blue eyes, and sweet faces.

I'm excited. I feel a providence running into the Scotts and now meeting Patricia.

I call Terry Johnson, the woman from the agency in San Francisco, as soon as I get home. Terry tells me she's not part of an agency; she runs a not-for-profit humanitarian organization.

"I had been working with many areas in Russia," she says, "but since I adopted my daughter, I only deal with Rostov, in southern Russia."

"Is it possible to get infants from there?" I ask.

"Because of all the bureaucracy in Russia," Terry says, "it's difficult to get a very young baby. But if you're really set on an infant, I could give you the name of a friend of mine here who deals with the Republic of Georgia."

I feel a twinge of disappointment. I want to work with this woman who sounds so sincere. I like that her organization is not-for-profit.

"Republic of Georgia?" I repeat, trying to remember exactly where that is.

"Yes," Terry says. "It used to be part of the Soviet Union. The advantage there is that you can get an infant and the babies never go to orphanages. The disadvantage to getting any infant, though, is that certain conditions might not be detected that could be seen in a slightly older child."

"I really want a young baby," I say.

"All right," Terry says, "You can call my friend, but she's in Europe right now. She'll be back in about two weeks."

* * *

March 11, 1996

I want to learn what I can about Georgia. I first stop at Barnes and Noble, but there isn't much on Georgia—mainly small sections about the Caucasus in travel books. Then I head to the Mid-Manhattan Library. The librarian suggests I start with the encyclopedia.

> Situated at the crossroads between the East and the West, Georgia has a rich and ancient culture, which can be traced back to prehistoric times. At varying times it has come under the control of the Roman Empire, the Byzantine and Persian Empires, the Mongols and the Turks, and in the last century, the Soviets.
>
> The roots of the Georgian people extend deep in history. Their cultural heritage is equally ancient and rich . . . with a literary tradition that dates back to the 5th century . . . The Georgians are a proud people. They have through the ages been noted as warriors as well as for their hospitality, their love of life, and their lively intelligence and sense of humor. The standard of looks is high, and many Georgian women belonged to the harems of the Ottoman sultans and the Shahs of Iran. The Georgians are also remarkably long lived.
>
> *Encyclopedia Britannica, Macropedia:*
> *Fifteenth Edition:*
> *Volume 28*

I remember a connection between Georgia and the Golden Fleece. I search out a book on mythology and find a section on Jason and Medea. Medea was the princess of Colchis, which I now realize, is modern-day Kolkhida, in Georgia. She was a priestess of Hecate, the goddess of the crossroads, and had magical powers. When Jason and the Argonauts came to her father's kingdom, Medea fell in love with Jason and used her supernatural powers to help him capture the Golden Fleece.

As I leave the library and walk amidst the skyscrapers in the cold March rain, I begin to feel fired up about this ancient place, thousands of miles away.

*   *   *

March 18, 1996

The woman who deals with Georgian adoptions still hasn't returned from Europe. Brian and I decide to go to a meeting sponsored by World Child, a not-for-profit adoption agency that has programs all over the world.

I ask about Georgia.

"I would not recommend it," the program director tells me. "The Georgian laws are extremely strict. It takes a very long time to get a baby, and once the baby is accepted, the adoption is final."

She recommends the Chinese and Vietnamese programs; with them, she says, it's relatively easy to get healthy infant girls.

*   *   *

March 23, 1996

I take the dogs and drive up to our country house in Garrison. Brian has stayed in the city to do a reading of a Tennessee Williams play. I open the sliding glass door on the back of the house to let the dogs out. They bark excitedly and dash up the hill and into the woods. I step out onto the cedar deck. The morning sun is shining and though the air is nippy, there's a feel of approaching spring.

I make myself a cup of tea and take it up to the loft. I get my world map and spread it out on the floor. I look at China, Vietnam, Russia, Poland, and finally—Georgia. I keep feeling myself drawn to Eastern Europe. Am I wanting somehow to return to that part of the world where my mother's family was uprooted?

I grew up knowing about my father's family, my French side, but the Polish side was something of a mystery. It was there, in my mother's heavy accent and in her intense emotionality. I knew that my mother's father had been a diplomat in Warsaw, that my mother's parents had been divorced, and that my grandfather had fled to France with his second family shortly before the Nazis invaded. I knew that my mother, grandmother, and great-grandmother had escaped from Poland during the war, and after fleeing to Italy and then Portugal, had wound up as refugees in Brazil. I came to understand, too, that my mother had run away from her mother to come to the United States, and didn't see her for twenty years. Much more than this, I didn't know. My mother would get angry when broached about the past.

It was not until my Polish grandmother found us through a private detective when I was sixteen that I began to acquire a sense of my Polish heritage. I loved hearing this elegant, highly dramatic woman tell stories of our "illustrious family." Whether the stories were real or made up, I didn't know, but at the time it gave me something of the identity I was starving for. Many years later, as my grandmother's memory slipped through the guardrails and began to speak for itself, she told me that my ancestry was Jewish. When I confronted my mother with this, she dismissed it as "nonsense." I began to fathom the immensity of this veil of secrecy under which I was raised. As my mother cut off from her past, something in her also cut off from me.

As a little girl, I adored my mother. I longed for her. But I could never be sure that she would be there for me; I always seemed to be in the care of other people. Even when my mother was with me, her gaze would go past me. Her eyes could never quite settle on me, see me. My earliest memories are of being sent away (to "good places," my mother would say). As I got older, she would go away—on her "extended" trips. I got used to her being away. Eventually, I even preferred it—her presence provoked so much anxiety.

In 1989, just a month before the Wall came down in Berlin, I went to Poland. I felt a sudden, overwhelming need to go. The events of the outside world were mirroring what I was feeling inside. I wanted the walls down. I wanted connection. If it wasn't possible with my actual mother, then at least within myself I needed to repair where things had gotten cut off.

I didn't find any traces of our family.

"I told you," my mother later said. "Everything was burnt—destroyed."

*   *   *

March 29, 1996

I finally reach Natasha at the adoption agency in San Francisco that deals with the Republic of Georgia.

"We have been very lucky with the babies out of Georgia," Natasha says in a slight East European accent. She speaks quickly, with a kind of crisp, savvy confidence that reminds me a bit of a theatrical agent.

"I heard it was quite difficult to adopt from there, that the laws are very strict," I say.

"Things have been getting tighter, but it's still possible. If you were to go with our program, I would probably offer you a boy first. Ninety percent of my clients want girls."

"I don't really care if it's a boy or a girl, as long as we get a healthy baby."

"So far, all the babies we have brought from Georgia have been very healthy," Natasha assures me.

"How young are they?" I ask.

"We have been able to get babies as young as two or three months. You always have the option to refuse the child, up to the very last moment, if for any reason you don't want it."

If we don't want it! I think to myself. *How could one see a baby and then refuse?* Yet I know I do feel better just having this option.

"I'll send you an application form," Natasha says. "By the way, have you done a home study?"

"A what?"

*   *   *

April 8, 1996

We do the home study. It's nothing like it sounds. You don't study anything. They study you—at home. It takes several hours. The counselor asks us all sorts of very personal questions about our marriage, our backgrounds, our religious beliefs, and our finances. Then she asks a series of hypothetical questions about how we would go about raising a child, how we would discipline the child, and so forth. Brian and I agree that we would tell the child as soon as possible about being adopted, and would teach him about his native culture.

We seem to have passed this test. The next step is the paperwork—reams and reams of it—everything from fingerprints to medical forms, letters of recommendation, financial statements, academic records, residency records, even police reports. All documents must have original seals and signatures. All of it must be notarized; all notarizations certified by the County of New York, and then all the documents must be apostilled by the state of New York for foreign governments. What on earth is an apostille?

*   *   *

April 10, 1996

We've made contact over the Internet with several couples who've adopted from Georgia. They sound extremely happy. We send in our application fee for the Georgian program.

* * *

April 11, 1996

Just as I'm waking up my shoulder dislocates. The pain is excruciating. I manage to push the joint back in the socket, but what a shock. This makes eleven times in five years. I have to do the surgery; I know it, but when, there never seems to be the time.

* * *

April 12, 1996

I meet with orthopedic surgeon, Dr. Pollack, at Columbia Presbyterian Hospital. He tells me the tendons are ripped off my shoulder, and urges me to have the surgery as soon as possible. He says he has an opening this Monday.

I decide to go ahead. I can't put it off any longer. I'll miss a day or two of teaching; I can make that up, but I'll have to use a sling for six weeks, and then there will be several months of physical therapy.

We were really hoping to do *In the Bedroom* this spring in the new Actor Studio Theater. This means it will have to be put on hold.

And the baby? How can I take care of a newborn baby with my arm in a metal brace? The doctor says it could be as much as a year before I have full use of my arm.

* * *

April 25, 1996

see if i can type this with my left hand. 10 days since the surgery. still in a lot of pain. the doctor says everything is o.k., just have to live through it. good thing i didn't think this through too much, i might not have done it . . . though eventually, i would have had no choice. went back to teaching right away. that felt good, even though i felt like collapsing after.

while in the hospital i had this amazing dream. i dreamt that brian and i were getting married. it was in a church that resembled a gothic cathedral in its ancient feeling and vaulted ceiling that reached high up into the sky. many people were at the wedding, including brian's parents, and my mother and

27

father. in reality, brian and i were married on a beach in cape cod with a small gathering of friends. brian's parents were there, mine were not. my father was deceased and my mother was in europe, unable to come. in the dream it was strange because I felt an invisible 'presence' hovering around and above us. brian slipped the ring on my finger and then i slipped the ring on his finger. and then suddenly i was aware of a baby in my arms. it felt so real—the three of us.

the next thing i remember i was giving my mother back the key to her apartment.

*   *   *

May 1, 1996

I come home from teaching; Brian meets me at the door.

"We had a son last week," he says nonchalantly, then turns and walks into the kitchen.

"What?" I say, unbuttoning my cape with my left hand, swinging it over my right shoulder with the clunky metal sling.

"The woman from the adoption agency phoned," he calls out. "She says she has a baby boy; if we're interested, she'll give us first choice."

I feel my heart skip a beat. "Born in Georgia?"

"Yeah, I guess," Brian says.

I drop the cape over the small Moroccan side table against the wall and go into the kitchen. A frying pan is on the stove, sizzling with oil.

"Are you joking?" I ask.

"No," Brian says, slicing a tomato.

"Did she say the baby is healthy?"

"I think so."

"What else did she say? Does she know anything about the parents?"

"I don't know." He throws pieces of eggplant and zucchini into the frying pan, making a loud crackling sound.

"Did she say how long it would take to get him?"

"No."

"So what did she say?"

"Not much, except that we have to decide by next week."

"Next week? What did you tell her?"

"I said that you would call her."

I try to calm myself, and then call Natasha.

"The baby weighs 7 1/2 pounds," she tells me. "A very good weight. We don't usually get such a good weight."

I get the sense that she's saying, "How can you refuse?"

She goes on. "Everything seems normal, for what we can see in so young an infant."

"Is there any information on the parents?" I ask.

"Usually, in these situations there is very little," she tells me. "I will have to see, but I am not really at liberty to do anything until you become a client."

* * *

May 8, 1996

We decide to say "no" to Natasha. I don't like it that she won't give us further information until we send her more money. It just makes me uncomfortable. The other reason is my shoulder; the physical therapist tells me to give myself at least three months before I take on a baby. Of course, it could take three months for all the papers to go through.

The truth is—I'm not ready yet.

* * *

June 27, 1996

I haven't spoken to Natasha since we said no to the baby. Secretly, I keep hoping that I'll get pregnant again, and that that will solve the issue of adoption.

But will it? Do I really want to get pregnant? When my period is three days late I panic. Is it fear of another miscarriage, or of *having* a baby? Maybe my mother is right. Maybe I'm not meant to be a mother.

I find myself watching Ingmar Bergman's "Persona" again, which concerns the relationship between an a star actress, played by Bibi Andersson, who has suffered a nervous breakdown and a young nurse, played by Liv Ullman, who has been assigned to her care. It brings up for me the whole issue of what it means to be an artist.

"Can you be two people at once?" Bibi Andersson's character asks Liv Ullman's.

I feel this incessant duality. Can one live an ordinary life and still be an artist? Can one really devote oneself to one's art and also have the time, the quality time, for a child? Does one creative process block another? Doesn't one side have to give in? And what are the compromises one has to make? Men do it all the time, but so often the children pay for it in one way or another. With a mother, it's even more fundamental. If a mother is not really present for her child . . . well, I know about that. One thing is clear. If I want a child, I'm going to have to *really* want it. It's going to take *effort* and *commitment*.

A Chance Encounter

July 1, 1996

I wander into the Whitney Museum and happen to run into Rena. We took a dream class together some years ago with Catherine Shainberg, a very gifted imagery teacher. Catherine was a protégé of the famed Israeli Cabalist, morphologist, and healer, Colette Muscat, and had studied with her for fifteen years in Jerusalem.

Rena and I didn't talk much outside of the class, but now, as we visit the Edward Hopper exhibit together, there's the sense of a bond between us. Maybe the dream work connected us more than I realized. Rena tells me about the difficulties she's had with her ailing mother, and I share with her my conflicts over baby. She tells me about Belinda, a psychic in North Carolina, who, she says has helped her tremendously.

"Catherine is the one who told me about her," Rena says. "Maybe you should give Belinda a call. She's not easy to reach, but keep trying. She might be able to help you."

Before we part, Rena scribbles down Belinda's number on the back of my museum ticket. I'm a little skeptical, but more than a little curious, and *desperate* to resolve this dilemma.

*   *   *

Belinda picks up the phone on the first ring. I'm thrown for a second, I was expecting to hear a recorded voice, but her manner is so friendly and receptive that it's easy to speak with her. I tell her about the miscarriages and about wanting to adopt, but I say I'm also feeling ambivalence about not having my own baby.

"I know I'm not pregnant," I tell her, "but I keep having images of child inside."

Belinda laughs. She has a warm laugh.

"I do see the possibility of a child coming soon," she says. "Before Christmas. I feel it's a very special soul."

I feel a sudden rush through my body that startles me with its intensity.

"But you have a choice," Belinda says. "If you decide not to adopt, the child will be okay and you will learn your lessons in another way."

My lessons? What does she mean by that?

"When I look at the little girl in your heart," Belinda continues, "she has a mother figure who is talking in the background. The little girl is trying to speak, but the mother figure is always talking, so there's not a connection . . . Your mother could not receive you. She couldn't see you. Maybe no one could see her. If I hear one word for you as a child, it's *lost*. You are now learning to be there for yourself. You are having to clear that old mother energy."

*　　*　　*

July 10, 1996

Ed Setrakian and his wife have just returned from Siberia with a fourteen-month-old baby boy.

"Everything went well," Ed tells me. "The baby is great."

"What are you calling him?" I ask.

"Edward Ilya Setrakian," Ed tells me.

I ask what he looks like.

"Like me," Ed says, laughing.

*　　*　　*

July 15, 1996

I tell Brian this morning that I'd feel much better about the adoption if I could meet with this Natasha in person. The whole thing is feeling way too abstract and impersonal to me.

Then today, she happens to call and leaves a message that she's going to Georgia on the twenty-sixth, and wants to know if we would be ready to receive a baby soon.

I call her right back. "Would it be possible to come to San Francisco to see you before you leave?"

There's a pause. I can hear that she's surprised by this request.

"Well . . . yes, of course," she says. "I'm going to be pretty tied up, but I would love to meet with you. Just let me know, and I'll try to make myself available."

* * *

July 23, 1996

Luckily, Natasha had to postpone her trip for a few days, which gave me time to make arrangements. Feeling excited to meet her, knowing she'll be in Georgia by the end of the week. On the bus to La Guardia Airport, I read an article about the terrible massacres in Rwanda and all the children now in orphanages, empty of hope.

If I could give hope and love to a child . . .

With so many children bereft of parents, without care and nurturing, without a home, it feels more right, somehow, to adopt than to try to force a pregnancy.

* * *

July 24, 1996, San Francisco

I enter a narrow, nondescript three-story building. I'm not expecting a fancy Spence-Chapin type of agency, but I am somewhat surprised by the *low-rent* look. I walk up two flights of stairs. At the top, I'm greeted by an attractive, young blond woman, with large blue eyes, wearing a flowered dress and high heels. She smiles, revealing dimples on both cheeks. This is Natasha? With her blond looks, broad face and colorful way of dressing, I have the immediate thought that she might be Polish. But mostly she looks so different than what I expected—softer, more feminine. I can't help telling her so.

"People are always surprised when they meet me," she says brightly. "I think they expect someone older and heavier. You look very different than I imagined, too. Younger, and less . . . formal."

"It must be this white jumpsuit," I say laughing.

She leads me through a hallway with bare walls. A dark-haired man pokes his head out of a room at the end of the hallway but quickly disappears. I suddenly have the feeling that I could be in Eastern Europe.

We enter a small windowless room.

"We can talk here," Natasha says, lightly. "Make yourself comfortable. I'll be back in a second; I want to give my assistant my portable phone so we won't be disturbed."

Is this her office? There's a desk, two chairs (one with a hole in the center), a small picture on the wall of some winter country scene, and, most noticeably, a bookcase with two rows of books on sales management. There is nothing in the room to suggest anything about adoption.

"How did you get into adoption?" I ask her when she returns, carrying two large albums.

"By accident!" she laughs. "I was studying law and working for an international business consultant when a friend of mine in Russia asked if I could help find them a baby. I had no idea, but I started inquiring. It would never have occurred to me to get into something like this, but once I started, I fell in love with the whole process. I will never forget the first time I went to an orphanage and saw all these toddlers coming toward me wanting to be taken."

"Here, I want you to see some pictures of the children," she says, placing a worn-looking album on the desk. She flips though several pages of adorable blond Russian children ranging from about one year old to six. But to my disappointment, there is only one page showing Georgian children. It's hard to see much from these few photos—whether because the pictures were not as well taken or because the babies are too young, I don't know.

"Will it be possible to get any information on the baby's background?" I ask.

Natasha shakes her head. "Usually in these situations there is not too much information available. Basically the mother relinquishes all rights in exchange for anonymity—often it's a case of an unwed woman who doesn't want her family to know about the child."

"But how do you know that there hasn't been abuse or alcoholism or mental illness?"

"That we do investigate," she says. "And all our babies are tested for AIDS and syphilis."

*   *   *

Natasha had warned me over the phone that we would only have a couple of hours together. We end up spending the entire afternoon together and then she invites me to dinner along with a colleague she is hosting from Bulgaria.

"We're taking you to a Georgian restaurant. The place might give you a feel for the Georgian look and manner."

I'm not sure how Georgian the restaurant is. It seems more a mixture of Russian and Armenian, but we are having a great time. I like the Bulgarian man, Leben. His English is limited, but we are able to communicate. Natasha and I are relating like best friends. She asks me to join her and Leben the following day. "I want to show Leben the wine vineyards in the Napa Valley," she says. "Have you been there?"

We never make it to the vineyards, but the countryside is beautiful and we end up spending much of the day in a luxury spa in Sonoma.

Water child that I am, I'm in heaven. Natasha lends me a bikini, and everything else is given by the spa—the robe, the slippers, the fruit and blossom shampoo and body cream, fresh fruits to eat, teas to drink. I'm enjoying this pampering.

"Don't tell my other clients about this," she says, giggling.

In the pool she asks about my acting and teaching.

"They'll be so impressed in Georgia," she says. "They'll think you're movie stars."

"Maybe they'll give me a job," I say, laughing.

Leben, who is now slouched on a chaise longue, has already decided that he wants me to give an acting workshop in Bulgaria.

By the time we return, it is after midnight. Natasha says it's too dangerous to take the subway back to Berkeley at this hour and insists I stay at her house. I accept the offer, more out of curiosity than fear of the subway. I sleep on the couch in a spacious, European-looking apartment. I open my eyes the next morning to find a cherub-faced, blond-haired little boy staring at me. I smile. He smiles back and runs away. He returns with Natasha's mother, a small, round elderly woman who doesn't speak much English and who looks very much from the old country.

*　　*　　*

July 29, 1996, New York City

I had such a positive experience in San Francisco, I left feeling excited and determined, Natasha said she would find me a "good" baby—so why do I feel ambivalent again?

"I think you will make a wonderful mother" is one of the last things she said to me. "You seem very together."

Appearances, appearances!

I wish I could go with Natasha to see those Georgian babies. How am I going to decide on a child by looking at a picture?

I call her now and ask if I can go.

"I'm afraid it's not possible," she says.

I speak very candidly to Natasha, in a way I never would have, had we not met and spent that time together. I share with her my ambivalence about career and family and my personal doubts that I will "have what it takes" to be a good mother.

Natasha listens sympathetically, but then her tone switches "back to business."

"You need to let me know before I go," she says, matter-of-factly. "Otherwise, I will leave your dossier in San Francisco."

I tell her to take our dossier.

I realize that with all this "should I, or shouldn't I" everything else is being pushed to the back burner. How can I even think about acting now?

*　　*　　*

September 6, 1996

It's been six weeks, and still no word from Natasha.

"Why hasn't she called us?" I complain to Brian.

"What if she has a baby?" he throws back. "You just started teaching a new class. You going to drop everything to go over there?"

*　　*　　*

September 13, 1996

As I come in from walking the dogs I see Brian hanging up the phone. "That was Natasha," he says. "She just came back; sounds like she was in Russia for quite a while. She says things are more open again in Georgia and that we will probably get a placement in about a month."

I need to speak with Natasha myself. But when I call her at home that night, she asks me to call her the next day at her office.

I call her office, but get her assistant. I leave a message. Natasha doesn't call back. It gets me angry.

*   *   *

September 14, 1996

I don't know if it's coincidence, synchronicity, or simply because we have our eyes and ears open, but it seems there's been so much in the media lately about adoptions. Last night Larry King did a special program on it. Jamie Lee Curtis was one of the guests. She's adopted a child and written a children's book about adoption. Loni Anderson and Leslie Abrams were also on. They've both adopted after having previously had biological children. Ronald and Nancy Reagan's adopted son, Michael, was on. He is now an adoption lawyer and advocate.

The emphasis on the program was the importance of telling the child about being adopted. The consensus was that it should be an open subject, and that there really is no difference in the love one feels for an adopted child versus a biological one.

Larry King quoted a good friend of his, who says, "I have four children; two are adopted and two are my own. I can't remember which is which."

John McCain, who was also on the program, adopted a child from one of Mother Teresa's orphanages in Bangladesh. He said he doesn't know anything about his child's biological parents and it doesn't matter to him at all.

*   *   *

September 15, 1996

Brian woke up this morning saying he had had a dream that he was pulling a baby out of me.

"I was delivering it," he said. "I was trying to convince the baby that it was okay to come out. That it was safe."

"And did everything go okay?" I ask. "Did it come out?"

"Yeah, sure," Brian says.

"Was it a boy?"

"I don't know," Brian says, and then adds with a smile, "but it was very little."

*   *   *

September 26, 1996

I finally reach Natasha and express my concern that she isn't returning our phone calls. I'm thinking that if I hadn't gone to San Francisco and met her personally, I might have already decided to use another agency and another program. She assures me that she hasn't forgotten about us.

*   *   *

That evening, Brian, our good friend Gary Swanson, and I do a reading of the Harold Pinter play, *Betrayal,* for Ted Mann, the artistic director of the Circle in the Square Theater, downtown. Ted is interested in working with us on the play.

*   *   *

October 11, 1996

Brian's birthday. We go to see our friend Lisa Richards in an Israel Horowitz play at the West Bank Café. After the show, we go out with Lisa and a few other friends, including Ted Mann and Gary Swanson. We toast Lisa on a terrific performance, and then toast Brian.

Everyone is rather surprised (but supportive) when we break the news of our plans to adopt a child. As the evening wears on, Brian and Gary are "feeling no pain," and get a little rowdy.

"To Georgia," Gary shouts, putting his arm around Brian and lifting him up out of his seat. "To the proud father!"

*   *   *

November 23, 1996

Still no placement from Natasha. I take Frenchie and Myshkin for a walk in the Park. It's a gray day, the ground covered with fallen leaves. I walk as far as the Delacorte Theater and then sit on a park bench overlooking the Great Lawn. *My mother* suddenly appears out of nowhere and sits a few feet away.

She looks dapper in her blue mohair hat, blue wool coat, and blue legging pants. She looks my way. She keeps looking, but gives no acknowledgment. Does she not recognize me? Have her eyes gone bad?

"Hi!" I finally call out.

I see a flicker of recognition.

"Oh," she says, flustered, "I'm dead. I just got off the plane."

She's returned from Switzerland, where she spends half the year. We end up walking together for a couple of hours. My mother is in a surprisingly light, amiable mood, and I'm succumbing to the moment of unexpected acceptance. We laugh about her not recognizing me. I even joke about another time when she didn't recognize me, many years before, when I was a teenager. I was at the Best Department Store, looking for a dress for my tenth-grade prom. I stepped into the elevator, and there was my mother. She stared at me, but did not see me. Her look was strange, distant . . . but not unfamiliar. It was the look that made me feel invisible.

"I could have walked out of that elevator without your ever seeing me," I say now, playing up the humor.

"Oh, that's not true," my mother says, with a giggle. "I know who my daughter is."

She calls me her daughter. Suddenly the barriers are down. Somehow, all the denial is worth this one moment. We're standing on the walkway that looks down on Bethesda fountain and the boat lake.

"What have you been doing lately?" my mother asks.

"I'm teaching at the New School," I say. "And Brian and I might be doing a play."

"That's nice," she says. "When?"

"I'm not sure," I say. "A lot depends on . . . we're thinking . . . about maybe adopting a baby."

I catch a look of surprise on my mother's face. I didn't intend to mention this; it just rolled out, somehow, in the openness of the moment.

"Oh?" she says, looking at me sideways.

Suddenly I feel the cold dampness of the air. "It's not definite yet," I add quickly, with feigned casualness. "We haven't even gotten a placement."

"Placement?"

"That's what the agency calls it when they have a baby for you to consider."

"And then you see the baby?" she asks.

"No. You get a picture," I say, forcing a laugh. "And then you have a few days to decide."

She smiles. "It's not even 'how much is that doggie in the window?' Do you find out anything about the background?"

"Not much," I say.

There is an uncomfortable pause.

"Well," my mother says, "I've always thought for the right people, adoption is a very good thing." Then with sudden vigor she says—"I heard of a terrible case recently. I think it was on the radio. These people adopted a child and . . ." A cyclist passes between us. I pull back Frenchie and Myshkin just in time.

"Well, anything can happen with one's own child, too," I blurt out, though fighting to maintain composure.

"Of course," she says. "Well . . . a baby will change your life."

*   *   *

December 10, 1996

Stress between Brian and me. We've been working on *Betrayal*, the Pinter play. It would have been better if Brian were playing the part of my lover rather than my husband. Anyway, whether it's the play or anxiety about the adoption, we both are extremely volatile right now.

*   *   *

Later, when we come home from rehearsal, there's a message from Natasha.

She says she has a baby.

*   *   *

A Boy

December 11, 1996

A boy! Born Oct 12th from an unwed mother in a small village south of Tiblisi, near the Azerbaijan border. The baby is half Georgian, half Azerbaijani. He weighs 10 lbs., has reddish-brown hair and large eyes. All his vital signs are normal. Tested negative for aids, syphilis, and TB. Head circumference 37 cm; chest 36 cm.

"His name is Kalipkul," Natasha says.

A beautiful name, Kalipkul, very musical, I think.

"This is all the information I have so far," Natasha goes on to say. "You will need to decide by next week."

"And then?"

"Then, if you decide you want him, it will probably take another six to eight weeks to process all the papers."

*   *   *

December 12, 1996

It's been two days. I haven't been able to think about anything but Kalipkul. Everything in my body feels alive and tingling.

A Libra. Born on the same day as Eleanora Duse, the great Italian actress . . . and Columbus Day—a sign for him to come to America! And a day after Brian's birthday. I'm just realizing that on the night of Brian's birthday, it was already after midnight when Gary was toasting Brian as the new father. It was October 12, and that was just as Kalipkul was being born. It gives me the chills.

*   *   *

I call Belinda, the psychic from North Carolina.

"Go to your knowing," she says. "Ask the child inside if it feels right. You've already made a karmic contract with the mother."

Another chill goes up my spine when she says that. I remember the dream I had last January about the woman handing me the baby. Could that possibly have been an image connected to Kalipkul?

"If it feels right to you," Belinda continues, "see yourself holding him. You're going to have the opportunity to give confidence, reassurance, protection, and support to the child that comes. He'll teach you to love the child within you."

*   *   *

December 14, 1996

The more I think about it, the more I'm sure I could say yes to the baby. Brian says he's fine whatever I decide.

Life is uncertain anyway, so why not take a leap?

But now Natasha is telling me to wait until we see his picture.

"You've been acting so nervous about this, I want you to be sure," she says. "We'll have a photo for you in about ten days."

"Would it be possible to make a videotape?" I ask.

"They don't do that for such small infants," she says. "And you wouldn't be able to see much anyway."

"We might be able to see *something*," I insist.

"They don't do it!" she says.

*   *   *

December 16, 1996

As I'm riding my bike downtown on the way to teach my class, I have a sudden thought. Georgia borders Turkey, and in Azerbaijan, their language is Turkic. What if we went to Turkey for the winter break? Maybe we could get a feeling for the baby's culture.

I find myself calling a travel agent.

*   *   *

December 17, 1996

We can't seem to get any more information about the baby from Natasha. She just repeats that he is fine, but does she know this for a fact, or is she just saying it to pacify me? I've been thinking that perhaps the mother is a Georgian woman who had a relationship with an Azerbaijani man—a "forbidden" in that society, from what I understand. My friend, Viviane, who is from Morocco and lived many years in Israel, says it's like an Orthodox Jewish girl having an affair with an Arab.

"But that gives you a better chance of getting a healthy baby," Viviane says, "if it's being given up because of social pressures, not because of alcoholism or drugs."

I wonder how much we will ever find out about the baby's background. Somehow, I don't feel that worried about it.

When I tell Viviane my idea of going to Turkey for the holidays to maybe get a feel of the baby's influences, she adds enthusiastically, "You should go to Israel. There are many Georgians living there."

*   *   *

At dinner, I say to Brian, "Did you know there are a lot of Georgians living in Israel?"

"No, actually, I didn't, he says, sensing something is up. "But did you know there are just swarms of Georgians living in Brooklyn? There's a very nice beach there, too."

"Stop joking, Brian. Anyway, Israel is closer to Georgia than Brooklyn. And maybe I can show the picture of the baby to Colette."

"Who?"

"Colette, the woman in Jerusalem who was Catherine's teacher. Catherine says she's absolutely brilliant at morphology. She must be getting very old, and this could be my last chance to meet her."

Brian leans across the table and breaks into a Bella Lugosi Dracula impression. *"Morphologically speaking, very interesting . . .* But what does it all mean?"

"Come on, you know, the study of the face, of form. If I showed her a picture of the baby, she could tell me what she saw."

"And?"

"I don't know. I feel it might be good to go and see her. It could be a kind of blessing. I've always wanted to meet her and I've always wanted to go to Jerusalem. This might be a perfect moment, right after seeing the baby—to go to the Holy Land."

*   *   *

December 20, 1996

I call Natasha and tell her we'd like the picture of the baby as soon as possible, as we would like to say yes.

"We might be going out of the country for the holidays," I say to her, thinking this might motivate her to hasten things.

"Where are you going?" she asks.

"Turkey, and maybe Israel from there."

"Go," she says. "Nothing's going to happen over the holidays anyway."

This is not the response I'm looking for.

"I hate to think of the baby lying there, waiting," I say.

"He's being well taken care of," she answers. "He's in our own care now, and he's getting special formula."

Then, a strange thing happens. I say, "You know, Georgia is just a few steps from Israel," to which she says, without any hesitation, "Well, you could go to Georgia and see the baby."

I'm stunned. "I could?" I didn't think this was a remote possibility. She herself had said so back in August.

"Normally we don't allow this," she tells me, "but I know how anxious you have been feeling, so just this once I may make an exception. I have to see when our coordinator will be there. I'll let you know on Monday."

*   *   *

I tell my class that I may be going to Israel during the break. "But my more important news," I say, "is that I might be adopting a baby."

"I dreamed about that," Deepak, my East Indian student from Canada cries out. "Don't you remember that I told you a while back that I dreamed that you had a baby? I'm very psychic that way."

*   *   *

December 22, 1996

I speak with another travel agent about flights to Georgia. I do think we're going.

Later at the New School speak with dean Lipton and tell him of our plans to adopt. He's extremely encouraging and shares with me that his wife was adopted. "And she's a real success story," he adds.

*   *   *

December 23, 1996

I phone Shelly Winters in Los Angeles to wish her a Merry Christmas. We did a film together some years back and we remained close; she's always been a big support for me. I tell her about the baby.

"You've given up on having your own?" she asks.

"Well . . ."

"If you adopt, then you'll get pregnant," she says, laughing. "Get the baby young.

"This baby is only two months old," I say.

"Well, get him as soon as possible. You don't know what they do over there. If there's abuse . . ."

"I don't think there's abuse," I say, now feeling worried, "but he may not be getting enough attention."

"That's abuse," Shelly says. "A baby needs to be held and cuddled."

*   *   *

December 24, 1996

Christmas Eve day. It's been two weeks and still we have no picture of the baby and no information as to when the chief coordinator will be in Tbilisi. We can't go to Tbilisi until she's there.

I feel terrible that the baby is just lying there, waiting.

Now Natasha says the chief coordinator might be staying in the States for a couple of weeks, though she doesn't know for sure. Everything is so vague. It's impossible to make an airline reservation without specific dates, especially at this time of year. I don't want to put off the decision on the baby until the middle of January. It means one more month that he'll have to be there. A month!

*   *   *

Later—I'm riding home on my bike, after some last minute Christmas shopping, when I see something peculiar. A brand-new baby carriage is lying on the sidewalk next to a large metal garbage bin. It seems so strange that it would be left here. I feel a sudden panic. Could someone have abandoned a baby? I look in and around the carriage. I try to lift the top of the garbage bin, but it's too heavy. I listen for any sounds that could be coming from inside the bin, but hear nothing. Suddenly, I'm aware of how dark and deserted this area is, and I don't feel safe. I get back on my bike.

I know I'm thinking about babies now and about babies that are abandoned; still, it seems odd that a nice new carriage would be left like this. I go straight home and call 911.

*   *   *

December 28, 1996

I've been listening carefully to the news and watching the newspapers, but I haven't heard word of any lost or abandoned babies. Thank God!

I'm still trying to contact Natasha. She doesn't seem to be anywhere where I can reach her. Boris, the travel agent, has made a reservation for us on Turkish Airlines for Wednesday, New Year's Day. He says if we don't take this flight, we'll have to wait another week.

*   *   *

December 30, 1996

How could I not think of it? I've certainly traveled enough in my life. Boris says we need visas to go to Georgia, and it takes at least two weeks to get them. He says we could pay three or four hundred dollars for rush processing, but it would still be impossible to get visas in the next few days because of the

New Year's holiday. In addition, Natasha needs to write a letter stating the purpose of our trip. Boris changes our reservation again.

Later, Brian phones the Georgian Consulate in Washington. It turns out that the visas don't have to take two weeks, and it won't cost three or four hundred dollars. We can get them in a few days for one hundred dollars each, but we do need the letter from Natasha.

*   *   *

December 31, 1996

The Georgian Consulate says if we don't send our application form and passports to them today, they won't be able to issue us visas in time for our flight next Sunday (we made another reservation with Boris, in spite of Natasha). "And we still have not received a letter of intention from your agency. If we don't receive that letter by Friday we cannot give you a visa."

All our material needs to be sent immediately via Federal Express. But where is Brian? He told me this morning that he was going to an audition, but that he'd be back at his office by 1:00 p.m. But I've been trying to reach him all day with no luck. Meanwhile, I can't send the package to the consulate without his passport photo. I try to busy myself sorting out clothes and items for the trip, but I'm getting terribly upset. Finally, I rush out of the apartment to go get my own photo taken. I feel like a crazy person as I weave in and out of traffic on my bicycle.

On the way home, I stop briefly at St. Paul's on Ninth Avenue. The church is empty except for a few homeless people. The lights are dim; soft medieval music is playing. I light a candle and sit for a few minutes. I know a part of me is thinking that maybe all these delays, lack of information, miscommunications, are a sign that this isn't supposed to happen. I pray for guidance.

I leave the church feeling better and evermore drawn to this baby, but then completely lose it when Brian comes home at 6:00. He's holding a bunch of flowers in his hand. He knows I'm furious, but he is trying to act as though nothing has happened.

"You know we're supposed to get all the material to the consulate," I say. "I must have called you fifteen times. Why would you make yourself so inaccessible when we're down to the wire?"

"I know you're upset," he says, "but the director twisted my arm to stay."

"Twisted your arm?"

"After I auditioned, he begged me to stay and read the play with the cast. I didn't know what to do . . . and then he offered me the role. Of course, I told him . . ."

"Life is choices," I snap back. "If this play is more important to you than a baby, just stay and do your little play!"

Eventually, I calm down. He had gotten his passport photo after all, and he did speak to the director about going to Georgia. He took my passport picture and all our materials and was able to get to the Federal Express Office just before they closed.

*   *   *

In the end, we do have a beautiful New Year's Eve. We go to the midnight celebration at St. John the Divine. Thousands hold their breath as a tightrope walker from France walks across the nave of the cathedral on a high wire. There is nothing below to catch him. The man seems to do this effortlessly, like an angel floating to the music of the spheres. It's an awesome performance of shapes, lights, music, and movement, telling the story of struggle and final victory!

Later, the singer, Odetta, leads the candle-lighting ceremony. One candle lights the next, illuminating the enormous space of the cathedral. As Brian lights the wick of my candle and I see the reflection in his eyes, I feel a serene peace and joy at what lies ahead.

*   *   *

January 2, 1997

Insensitive of me not to consider Brian's feelings about the play. Of course, he wants to do it. While he's out walking Myshkin and Frenchie, the director calls.

"I really would like Brian to do the part," he says.

"And Brian wants to do it," I say. "It's just that we have this problem."

"I don't consider that a problem," he says. "I see it as a good thing."

So he understands about the baby!

Brian should do the play: I don't want to be the cause for him missing out on an opportunity. The play is a reality; the adoption is a possibility.

After all, we still don't even know if we're going to Georgia. And then I could always go alone.

* * *

I meet an attractive, middle-aged Russian couple in the park. They seem quite familiar with Georgia. The woman tells me that Tbilisi is a beautiful city and that the Georgians are a very warm, generous people.

"But watch out for the men," the man says, with a knowing smile.

* * *

Back home, I re-read the travel advisory Natasha sent us:

> The Republic of Georgia in the Caucasus Mountains reminds us of the American Wild West. Law and Order have yet to come to this land, which has been split by ethnic fighting, and plagued by organized crime. During the Soviet years, Georgia was the top destination in the region, offering magnificent monasteries, a beautiful seacoast, historic sites, scenic mountains and renowned food and drink. While the sights are still there, the bitter separatist struggle between the government of Georgia and its breakaway republic of Abkhazia has made the country too unstable for casual tourists, and we predict it will be for some time to come.

* * *

January 3, 1997

I come home from the health club feeling relaxed after a long swim. Brian has reached Natasha. "The coordinator is in San Francisco," he tells me, "but Natasha says she can't tell us anything until she knows when the coordinator is leaving."

"Did you tell her how we've had to cancel our reservations five times?"

"She says there's nothing she can do about it. She says the travel agent is used to that."

"Did you ask her if we could maybe speak with the coordinator ourselves?"

"I must be a mind reader," Brian says. "I knew you'd ask me that. "She said she couldn't reach the coordinator."

My relaxation is starting to go. "*Couldn't reach her? Why?* How does she communicate with her? And what about the baby's picture?"

Brian throws his hands in the air in a gesture of exasperation. "Maybe you should speak with her."

When I try to call, I can't get through to her, though. That's probably a good thing. I just might have told her to forget about everything and that we would look for someone else to work with. That would be totally stupid of me, and that's not what I want, but I'm in such a rage.

The good thing that comes out of my fury is that I also call World Child—the not—for-profit adoption agency in New York, and they put me in touch with Heather, a single mom who's adopted a baby from Georgia. She soon returns my call and couldn't be warmer or more enthusiastic. I've noticed that adoptive parents seem to be very generous about helping others who are going through the process. She tells me she used a private lawyer for her adoption. She had planned to stay three weeks in Tbilisi but ended up staying three months before she could bring her baby girl home.

Heather wants me to speak with another friend, Tom, who has also adopted from Georgia, and during our conversation, she makes a conference call to him. He and his wife adopted an infant boy from Georgia a year before Heather adopted her daughter. Tom is clearly in love with his son, who is now close to three. He is more than happy to speak with me, but his tone is far more ominous.

"Tbilisi is not a place where you want to spend any more time than you have to," Tom says. "It's like nowhere else you've ever been."

Heather agrees. "Tom had warned me that when you leave Moscow and go to Tbilisi, it's like falling off the edge of the earth. And it is true. I've been to a lot of third world countries, but this is much worse."

"It's chaos," Tom says. "Do *not* go alone. Believe me, kidnapping for ransom is not uncommon there."

"But Heather was there alone," I say.

"Yeah, but she first had her lawyer behind her and then the American embassy . . ."

Heather cuts in, "Well, I don't know, as long someone picks you up at the airport, and you always have someone with you when you go out . . ."

"If you go," Tom continues, "don't stay in a private home. And it really would be better not to go in winter, because of all the shortages. There's no electricity or heat in the winter.

How can I let the baby wait there until the weather gets warmer? I think to myself.

"I went in December," Tom goes on, "and the only place to get a little warmth was my hotel, because they had a generator. It's also safer in a hotel; they've got soldiers with machine guns at the entrances."

My head is swirling. This sounds so much worse than I anticipated—poor, yes, but not uncivilized.

Despite this rather frightening picture, in the end, they don't discourage me from getting a baby from Georgia.

"All the babies I've seen from there, and I've seen about ten now, have been very healthy," Tom says.

"And they're beautiful babies," Heather adds. "I've really investigated different countries and I think there's a much better chance of getting a healthy baby from Georgia. The people are strong, and the women don't drink or smoke or have illicit sex. There's no AIDS."

This confirmed what Natasha had said, that the babies are usually given up for reasons of poverty, or because of a young girl getting pregnant out of wedlock.

*   *   *

That evening I meet Brian at Hunan Park, our neighborhood Chinese restaurant, and tell him about my call to Heather.

"I don't want you to go alone," he says emphatically. "I'll tell them I can't do the play."

"No," I say. "You're committed now. They're depending on you. I'll be fine. You think if people were kidnapped or killed off while adopting children, adoption agencies would be able to stay in business?"

"Yeah, if they have good lawyers, sure."

"Oh, come on, Brian."

"All right then, but you have to promise me to be extra careful and not go anywhere alone."

*   *   *

January 4, 1997

I visit Heather and her daughter, who's now eighteen months old. Heather is probably in her mid-forties by the way she describes herself, but looks mid-thirties. The little girl, Caroline, is adorable—very outgoing and playful. She has large hazel, almond-shaped eyes, light brown hair, and a smiling face. It's so beautiful to see the love between mother and child. Heather tells us of the ordeal she went through to bring Caroline home.

"I was basically under lock and key for three months," she says, "because shortly after I arrived in Tbilisi, a moratorium went into effect."

"What do you mean, a moratorium?" I ask.

"There was some kind of governmental decree against foreign adoptions. My lawyer told me that if anyone discovered why I was there, I'd have to leave the country and I'd never get my baby. I couldn't even go outdoors unless he was with me. I didn't want to do anything to jeopardize my chances of getting the baby. It was a nightmare."

Heather lifts Caroline onto her lap and holds her close. "I thought I'd go insane," she goes on. "But now, if I had to, I'd do it all over again. I've wanted a little girl for so long, but I know it's not by chance that I got Caroline. It's funny, when you're about to get a child, you worry so much about all the changes and adjustments you're going to have to make in your life, and that's true, but it's the inner changes that are really incredible and surprising."

*   *   *

When I get home the passports have arrived from the embassy. They waived the letter of intention from Natasha and gave us visas to enter Georgia. Despite the State Department warning, I'm still willing to go alone, but it doesn't look as though it's going to be on Sunday. I also don't know about going to Israel now. In Hebron, an Israeli attacked and seriously wounded six Palestinians, and CNN is warning that tourists could be targets for terrorist attacks.

*   *   *

January 5, 1997

When I come in from walking the dogs there's a message from Natasha on the answering machine. She says she wants to touch base with me and that she'll give me an update when we speak.

Then there's a long message from Terry. "Natasha received a photo of the baby yesterday," she says, "and she'll be sending it right off to you."

Natasha received a photo? *That's odd; why didn't she mention this in her message?* I wonder. And then, the biggest surprise—"You can leave for Georgia as soon as you like."

I can?

Terry's message continues. "Once you have your baby, this will seem like a distant dream, but I know when you're in the middle of this, it can seem quite frightening."

Terry's last words are to wish me the best on my trip. "I hope that when you get to Georgia, you will find that this baby is just the right one for you."

I play the message over and over again. I feel my prayer has been answered.

*   *   *

While Brian is rehearsing, I visit my friend Didi, who is an adoptive mother, at her house in Sneeden's Landing. Her friend, Janet, is also there. Didi gives me a little stuffed Dalmatian to bring to the baby, and a diary to record my trip and jot down any questions I might want to ask. "You'll want to know what the baby is being fed?" Didi says. "How much? How often? How many babies are there in the ward? How many nurses or caretakers are there?" She suggests bringing a warm blanket for the baby; maybe several, in case there are other babies there who need them. Janet, who's also a mom, says that I might want to bring formula.

These are mothers talking. I'm so grateful for their suggestions. But when I get home, I break into sobs. I suddenly feel so naïve and lacking that I hadn't thought of these things myself. I feel ungenerous.

At midnight, Natasha calls. Her tone is friendly and personal.

"Tell me the arrival time in Tbilisi so that I can let Dodo, my coordinator know," she says.

It's clear she is making an effort. She tells me I'll be met at the airport and taken to a hotel; then to the hospital to see the baby. The coordinator will try to arrange a "home-style" hotel for me, "if there's room," she says.

"I didn't know there were so many tourists this time of year," I say, lightly.

"It will probably cost $65 per night," she goes on. "But the main hotel will cost $250 a night."

"Two hundred fifty dollars? For what?" I ask.

"Exactly," she says, with a laugh. "And you would not believe what they charge for a little room in Moscow! Now, the rules of the hospital are that you can only stay with the baby an hour and a half—maximum."

"Would I be able to go back the next day?" I ask. "I'm going to be there for at least a few days."

"We'll try to get special permission, but I cannot promise."

Then, almost as an afterthought, Natasha adds, "oh, and I have received the photo."

I catch my breath. I want to ask how the baby looks but instead find myself asking, "Have you sent it?"

"Not yet," she says.

"Could you send it on Monday?"

"But you're leaving on Monday."

"Well, I don't know if that's possible now. I may be leaving Thursday."

"Then I'll send it," she says. "The baby looks very cute. I know it sounds corny, but he even looks a little like you. I'm sure you're going to fall in love with him."

I feel giddy with excitement. I want to talk more about the baby.

Natasha's tone abruptly changes. "Now, I have to tell you one more thing. You're dealing with a very dangerous situation here. We're allowing you to go see this baby, but what happens after, we can't be responsible for."

I think at first, she must mean she can't be responsible for my life. That I could be assaulted, kidnapped, sold into white slavery. But then I realize she's saying she cannot be responsible for what the Georgian government might do.

"This program could shut down at any moment," she says. "You have to be prepared emotionally for that. You could say yes to this baby, and then things could be delayed, or the laws could suddenly change, and there would be nothing we could do. You have to be prepared for that possibility."

Didi had said something similar. Not about the program shutting down, but about the fact that if we see the baby and want him, we have to be prepared for the pain of leaving him, maybe for some time, until we can take him home.

"The baby is an abstraction now," Didi said, "but once you see him . . ."

*   *   *

January 6, 1997

I wake up this morning with a kind of undefined angst in the pit of my stomach. I know it's not that I'm afraid to go to Georgia alone. It's that Brian is willing to let me go alone—that he's willing to let me make the decision about the baby, alone.

"How can you not care more?" I say a little too casually as he sits having breakfast, before heading off to rehearsal.

"What are you talking about?" he says, glancing at the open newspaper in front of him.

"The baby," I say. I pour milk into my tea and stand by the kitchen counter. "Letting me decide."

Brian looks up. "You're the one who told me to stay." There's an edge of defensiveness in his voice. "I wanted to go, remember?"

"Oh come on, just because I told you to stay."

"Look, you want me to go, I'll go," he says.

"No, what do *you* want?" I cry, accidentally knocking over my tea, which goes crashing to the floor. "Oh shit!"

Brian moves to help me.

"Leave it. I'll do it," I say, pushing his hand away and grabbing a roll of paper towels to soak up the mess.

"Fine," he says. He goes for his jacket and hat. "Look, I'm late for rehearsal."

"You don't seem to care about the baby. You care more about a silly little play. If you don't want to go through with this, I'll adopt him on my own."

"I'll call you later," he says. The door slams shut.

I've been convincing myself that it would be fine for me to go alone. Whatever altruism there has been in this thought, it has been fed by some fantasy of heroism, of venturing off alone into the wilderness to rescue a child who has been abandoned by the world. The truth is we have to do this together. If we start off separately, with this—the most important decision of our lives, how can we ever hope to be a family? Brian has been taking such a backseat in this whole thing. "Whatever you decide will be fine with me," he keeps saying. I want him to have a stake in this, too.

* * *

Brian calls during his lunch break. "I've checked into it," he says. There's urgency in his voice. "If I fly by way of Moscow, I can get a flight back the same day and not miss too much rehearsal. Even if I'm there just a few hours, it's worth it."

"I appreciate the thought," I say, coolly, "but it will be exhausting, very expensive, and we won't even be traveling together. What would be the point?"

"We would see the baby together," he says.

I hear him telling me he does indeed care, but I'm finding it hard to surrender. "No," I say.

"Well, I'm going to see what can be done," he says and hangs up.

In spite of myself I call Boris to find out what's possible, and then call Brian at rehearsal.

"If you can fly the eighth and be back in New York on the fourteenth, we could fly together by way of Istanbul."

"Let's see what I can do," he says. There's softness in his voice. There's softness in both our voices.

Fifteen minutes later, he calls back.

"It won't work for the director. The show opens Wednesday. The only possibility is Moscow."

I can feel the anger rising again. "Can't they just postpone the opening for two days?" I ask. "I mean you're willing to be back for them. They know the situation. Can't they give a little?"

"He told me last night that if I quit, he'd cancel the show."

"You're not quitting," I say. "You're just trying to make it all work. They've got to have some understanding. Anything can be changed, especially if they really want you."

"Okay," he says with a sigh. "I'll talk to him once more."

Poor Brian. He's getting it from all sides.

An hour later, he calls again.

"I can go. They'll delay the opening till I get back."

*　　*　　*

January 8, 1997

I'm still half asleep, trying to write house-sitting instructions for my sister-in-law, when Brian dashes into the study. He's got a half-torn Federal Express envelope in his hand.

"Look!" he says excitedly, thrusting a photo at me.

I'm struck by his energy and enthusiasm. There's no hesitation. I feel a rush as I take the picture. I look at a close-up of the baby.

"He's beautiful," I cry.

In my dreams, I had seen him beautiful this way, but with the long delay of the picture, I had started to wonder if there was something wrong.

"He's adorable," Brian says.

We can only see the face. The rest is bundled up in a white blanket and a white cap with orange flowers on it. He has a very open face—large, alert, dark eyes; the right eye a little more open and focused than the left. His skin looks fair, reddish, but that could be the photo processing. What I'm noticing most of all is the nose. Broad, with the nostrils nicely open.

"He's got your nose," I say to Brian.

Brian beams.

Instant parents! (Like what they call "overnight success," though one overlooks the life it took to get to this point.)

"He doesn't look too underfed," I say, going by the roundness of his cheeks.

"No," Brian says.

Anyway, Kalipkul looks perfectly normal and content. He has an expression of both calm and curiosity. He almost seems to be asking, "Why are you taking a picture of me?"

I feel so tempted to call Natasha right away and say "yes," but now the trip is all arranged. We're leaving in just a few hours.

"You might reach her more easily from Georgia, anyway," Brian jokes.

Have to rush. There's still so much to do. Brian will be at rehearsal till the last minute.

I phone my mother to say goodbye.

"Oh, you haven't left yet?" she says. "I'm sure you will have a wonderful time." Light, easy, as though I were off to buy a hat!

Georgia

January 10, 1997

I hear a loud rumbling sound and feel a vibration at my feet.

"It's the landing gear" Brian says, "It's okay."

We look out the window and see only blackness. Are we going to land without runway lights? I wonder. I clutch Brian's hand and pray for the pilot's expertise. A sudden driving rain beats hard against the window. I say another prayer—this time for us. Finally, a small group of lights and a *tiny* runway come into view. Another loud rumble and we touch ground. Everyone claps. We've made it to Tbilisi!

In the dark rain we follow the crowd across the holding area into a small, dimly lit building that looks more like a bus station than an airport terminal. Inside, the crowd quickly bunches up behind the customs agent who is sitting at a desk. They all seem to be familiar with this place as they nudge their way past us to get in closer to the agent. Behind him is a gate where a small group waits to greet arriving passengers. I'm wondering which one of them is the coordinator. As we get closer, I catch sight of a young woman with thick, dark eyebrows. She's at the gate, leaning over the railing, trying to see the names on the passports being examined by the customs agent. Her face looks exceedingly strained. I have the feeling that she's here for us, but it's only when our passports are in the official's hands that she looks in our direction. She looks back at the passports, back at us, and abruptly smiles. Ten years seem to drop off her face. She leans toward the official and whispers something. After several minutes of discussion between them, the official gives us one more studied look and stamps our passports.

"This way," the young woman says with a slight accent, quickly steering us away from the line.

"Are you the coordinator?" I ask.

"No, I am interpreter," she says. "My name is Eke."

"You speak English very well," I say.

"Thank you. I studied at school. Come. You have luggage?"

A white-haired, neatly dressed older man meets us outside.

"He is driver," Eke tells us.

"Is the coordinator here?" Brian asks.

"She was not able to come," the young woman tells us. "She will see you tomorrow at hospital."

We've been traveling for twenty-eight hours. I should be exhausted, but I feel excited and wired. I wish we could go see the baby right now.

We drive slowly for a long time along a completely dark road. The car has only one dismal headlight; it's impossible to see more than a few feet ahead through the fog. I try not to think about it, but it does occur to me: "Are we being kidnapped?"

Brian breaks the long silence. "How is the political situation in Georgia now?"

I give him a sharp nudge. We've been specifically warned not to talk about politics, and so what is the very first thing out of his mouth? But Eke responds immediately, "It is better," she says. "But still we have many problems. It was terrible two years ago. There was war only a few hours away in Abkhazia. People here went crazy. It was very dangerous. Still, it was better than during Soviet period. At least we are independent now. Now we have chance to rebuild."

She goes on, unprompted by questions. She is eager to talk and tells us about the refugee problem. "It is terrible," she says, "we have a half million refugees in Tbilisi."

After a good hour, we finally pull up in front of a house.

"This is your hotel," Eke says.

In the darkness, we stumble through a gate and go up some steps. Our driver knocks on a door several times. *Can anyone hear us?* I wonder. We wait for what seems a long time. Then a man opens the door. He's wearing a robe and slippers and looks half asleep. He's holding what look like two battery-operated lanterns.

"He is the owner of the house," Eke tells us. "He says he is sorry there is no heat or light."

We make a sign not to worry.

It's now about 3:30 a.m. We are given one of the lanterns, and the owner leads us up a flight of stairs.

"Your room is here," Eke says, pointing to the room on the left.

We open a heavy wooden door into a large room. In the half-light, it looks quite elegant, with decorative wallpaper, heavy drapes, and two beds placed together side by side. There's also a nice-sized bathroom. We're told there's no hot water, but there are towels and toilet paper.

This is so much more than we expected.

*   *   *

It's 11:00 a.m. I kick off the cover and scramble out of bed. I'm worried we may have slept too late. Today we see the baby. I feel a surge of nervousness and excitement as I pull off my nightgown and quickly throw on some fresh clothes. I notice that our room is much warmer than it was last night. The electric heater on the floor is flaming red. I try the light; it's working.

I pull aside the two layers of heavy red felt curtains that cover the bedroom window. It's a cool, gray, wet morning. We're on a narrow street, looking across to a house with bars on the windows. I open our window a crack; the air feels fresh and moist.

"Brian . . . Brian, wake up. We're in Georgia!"

*   *   *

Downstairs, heavy drapes are still drawn, allowing only a small spill of light to enter. A woman with black hair, thick dark brows, and a thin nose is sitting in an armchair in front of a small television set. Her body is slouched, her elbow on the arm of the chair, her fist pressed against her chin. She looks asleep, but as we reach the bottom of the stairs, she suddenly springs to her feet. She smiles shyly, and gesturing for us to follow, leads us through a dark hallway into a spacious, country-style kitchen.

There's a huge breakfast on the table—bread, sausage, cheese, figs, yogurt, halvah, orange juice, different kinds of cakes, cornflakes, and pate. There's even a bottle of champagne. *Is this all for us?* I wonder.

The woman holds up a couple of eggs and points to a frying pan. We smile and shake our heads; there's already so much to select from. We feast more with our eyes and curiosity than with our mouths. We can't wait to finish breakfast to phone Eke. We're so eager to see the baby and meet the mysterious coordinator.

"Coordinator will pick you up in one hour to take you to hospital," Eke tells us over the phone in the downstairs hallway.

While Brian returns to the kitchen to study his lines (he has to seize any moment he can), I explore the house. There's a large salon with a piano, a fireplace, elegant wood furniture with velvet upholstery, and flowing drapes of delicate brocade. Paintings cover almost every inch of the walls—expressionistic portraits and striking theatrical scenes. I feel drawn to them. They seem to confirm my belief that Georgians are a very artistic people.

Two television sets, the one downstairs and one in the owner's bedroom, drone on, although nobody seems to be watching. *It's odd,* I think. *We've been told this is a hotel, but I don't see any other guests.*

I throw on my jacket and step outside. It's damp and chilly. I walk down the steps to the street and turn back to look at the house. It looks freshly painted—bright yellow with orange trim—and stands out starkly against the other buildings, which are gray and seem badly in need of repair. The hotel looks almost like a movie set compared to its surroundings.

I venture down the dirt road. The further along I walk, the more deterioration I see. Heaps of rubble is everywhere, and there are many buildings with charred exteriors and broken windows.

I pass a few old women. One stands behind a cart, selling cigarettes. She is short, squat, and dressed in a dark worn coat with a black wool scarf tied around her head. She gives me a quick, intense look, and then just as quickly averts her gaze. There is the same reaction from the two other old women I see. I turn a corner and suddenly find myself in a desolate, deserted-looking area. There's a gigantic mound of garbage in the middle of the street. I see scraps of metal and glass, broken furniture, pieces of mattress, a smashed windshield. There's an eerie silence that suddenly feels threatening. I'm sure I shouldn't be wandering here alone. I head quickly back to the hotel.

*   *   *

A tall, large woman with bleached-blond hair and heavy features is standing at the door with Brian.

"I am coordinator," the woman says in a husky voice, extending her large hand.

My immediate feeling is that she looks a little coarse to be handling babies.

"We will go?" she says, pointing to the small, rusty car parked in front of the house.

I try to get in, but the door won't open.

"I am sorry, is broken," the woman apologizes, "everything in Georgia is broken."

She pounds the lock with her fist and then forcefully yanks the door open.

Brian and I crawl into the tight backseat.

"Are you Dodo?" I ask, once she has managed to get the car started.

"I am Dr. Ivana Vasaladze," she says, looking up at me through her rear view mirror. "Dodo is second name. I do not like this name, but everybody calls me this."

"What would you like us to call you?" I ask.

She laughs, a surprisingly hearty laugh. "Okay, call me Dodo," she says. "Because if you call me Ivana, I will not know to whom you speak. Ivana is official name."

"Anyone with a name like Dodo can't be all bad," Brian whispers in my ear.

I'm thinking she looks more Russian than Georgian, but when I ask her, she says, "Georgian. Absolutely."

Brian gives me a nudge. Yes, it was probably not a very polite question to have asked, though Dodo laughs it off. She seems to laugh easily. I don't remember being told that our coordinator was a doctor.

"Are you a pediatrician?" I ask, leaning forward so she can hear me above the raspy engine.

"No," Dodo says. "I am specialist for diabetes."

I think of the large box of chocolates that we've brought her as a present.

Dodo patiently tries to answer our questions about the baby. She tells us that he's had an Apgar test—a standard medical test of a newborn's well-being—that all his results are normal, and that his health is good. Then she says he was born in Tbilisi, not Mariuli, as we'd been told.

"Not Mariuli?" I say, surprised.

"They say Mariuli," she explains, "because in Mariuli live people who are Azerbaijani and baby is half Azerbaijani."

"How do you know?" Brian asks.

"Because his family name is Azerbaijani," she says.

"So the father is . . . ?" I ask.

"The mother is Azerbaijani," Dodo goes on. "The father is Georgian. Baby has mother's family name—not Georgian."

"Does he look more Georgian or Azerbaijani?" I ask.

"Georgian!" she says, with proud emphasis. "Absolutely."

We drive for what seems like hours. I wonder why we are staying in a hotel so far from the hospital. Was there no choice? As we pass row upon row of tall, dilapidated, Soviet-style tenement buildings I'm reminded of Poland as it looked when we saw it in 1989. It was during the collapse of the Communist system.

We continue beside a wide, fast-moving river. I ask Dodo the name.

"We call it Mtkvari," she says, "but on maps is Kura. Is Russian name of Mtkvari. Different names—Georgian and Russian."

There are no more houses here to the left, but we pass a towering monument of a hammer and sickle, the Soviet symbol of Communism. I am surprised that it is still standing.

"If we say yes, how long will it take to get the baby?" I ask.

"They say they need one more paper for sign—for adoption process. But now government stop everything for about two weeks."

"Stop the adoption process?" I say. I look to Brian.

"Not stop," Dodo quickly says. "How you say?"

"Slow down?" Brian offers.

"Yes," she says, "slow down and make a little longer."

"So how long do you think it will take?" I ask again. "Altogether?"

"I do not know yet," she says. "I think beginning of February everything will be ready. When government say yes, it will finish then very fast."

We come to a stop in front of an iron gate.

"This is Republic Children's Hospital," Dodo tells us, pointing to the building in front of us, a two-story, block-like cement structure with small windows.

My heart pounds wildly as we get out of the car.

Tattered sheets and children's clothing flap on a clothesline over a scraggly lawn. The rear part of the building looks like a big black hole—as if it could have been bombed. I look around and see other such buildings in the distance. Large, misshapen cavities stand out in sharp relief.

"Are those parts of the hospital?" I ask Dodo.

"Yes, but mostly for refugees to live now."

Sudden bright sunshine blinds me, and I stop. I would like to ask about the refugees. I'd also like to linger a moment in the sun. I don't feel ready to go into the hospital; I'd like to take a walk first. Or maybe a run.

"Come," Dodo says.

I can't tell her I don't want to go in yet. I've pushed so hard to get here.

Two emaciated dogs, one missing its front right leg, dart from behind the bushes. One pauses a moment to look up. He's young, with large, questioning eyes, and ears that flop over at the tip. Pretty, if it weren't for a drab gray coat and ribs protruding sharply under thin skin. I take a step toward him; he cowers and slinks back out of sight.

"Who do the dogs belong to?" I ask.

"Nobody," Dodo says. "Is problem. Too many dogs in Tbilisi."

We follow her up the broken steps. Inside, we enter a stairwell. With the light gone, surrounded by crumbling cement, the air feels cold and raw. A musty claylike smell seems to emanate from the walls. We stop in front of a door with chipped, opaque glass. Dodo knocks, but the sound is swallowed by the thick partition. She knocks again, harder this time.

She looks around at me with a resigned smile. "We must wait," she says.

The door opens. A woman in a white coat with dark hair and the now-familiar thick brows looks first to Dodo, and then to us. She slowly opens the door wider and gestures for us to enter. We step into the middle of a long hallway. It takes a moment to adjust to the darkness. I can hear voices and the crying of babies, but the hall looks empty. Dodo introduces the woman as the head doctor of the ward. I smile. The smile is not returned. Dodo continues to speak with the doctor in Georgian. The doctor listens, but keeps her eyes fastened on me. Did she know we were coming? Does she like that we are here? It doesn't feel so. I don't know what to do except return her gaze and try to stay as open as possible. She is dark, reserved, and steely. Dodo suddenly seems our best ally.

Two women wearing white coats emerge from a room, carrying metal pails. They take us in, but also do not smile. I wonder if word has gotten out that the foreigners have arrived. The women walk down the gray hall and enter a room. When they open the door, I hear the wailing of a baby. Its screams sound hysterical. Brian and I look to each other.

A wave of fear sweeps through me. We had been told before we left New York that the baby had caught a little cold, but was fine. I begin to imagine something's gone wrong. That maybe he isn't fine. Maybe he's very sick. Maybe that's why the chief doctor is looking so serious.

"We will go," Dodo suddenly announces.

I move toward the right.

"No, this way," she says, heading left.

I hadn't noticed, but the chief doctor has gone. I quicken my step. "Is there a problem?" I ask, catching up to Dodo.

"No problem, no problem," she says. "We will see baby now."

We will see baby now I hear echo in my head. My worry for the baby switches to panic for myself. This is no longer an idea, a fantasy, or an abstraction. We're about to see a real, live baby. We're about to make a decision that will affect the rest of our lives.

We come to a kind of alcove. Another woman in a white coat comes up to Dodo. We stop as the two speak. This woman does smile at us. I smile shyly back. I'm like a child entering a new school, grateful for even the smallest sign of acceptance.

A weathered, artificial Christmas tree stands crookedly in the center of the alcove; a few paper ornaments dangle miserably from the frayed branches. A young woman dressed in a worn overcoat with a scarf around her head is sitting on a nearby wooden bench. She is holding a tiny bundle in her arms. The woman glances at us, but then immediately lowers her eyes. Behind her, through a window, I can see the sheets blowing frantically in the wind. It looks as though the sun has gone.

I wonder if the woman's baby is sick. Maybe it is just here for a check-up. Or, could it be, possibly, that the woman is here to give up her baby? I wish she would look our way again. I want to see her face.

There is a bulletin board on the wall, opposite to where the woman is sitting.

"Let's look," I say to Brian, pulling at his hand.

We step closer to the woman. She does not look up. On the board are pictures of babies ranging from what look to be a few months to a couple of years. It is hard to tell much from their expressions. It is the nurses holding them who are providing the smiles.

"I am ready," Dodo says, coming up behind us.

We turn and follow her past the Christmas tree.

"A sad tree," Dodo says.

We continue down the long hallway.

"Where is the baby's room?" I ask.

"At the end," Dodo says.

The hallway becomes narrower and darker; the crying louder now. My hands are wet against Brian's dry palms. I can feel my heart pounding again.

What if I can't do this? What if I don't feel anything when I see him? What if I don't want him?

I stop abruptly.

"Is there a bathroom . . . ?" I ask.

Dodo looks back at me. Does she see the terror on my face?

"Of course," she says. "We must ask. You wait."

She disappears back down the hall.

My legs feel weak. "You don't want to come back tomorrow?" I ask Brian, only half joking.

"What's wrong?" he asks.

"Oh, nothing. Jitters. Maybe it's jet lag."

"We don't have to make the decision today, you know."

"I know," I say. But I know I will make the decision today.

"You're going to be fine," Brian says, putting his arm around me. "You're a warrior, a miracle worker. Look how you've managed to get us this far."

A warrior maybe, but a mother?

Dodo comes back with a short, squat old woman in a gray uniform. The woman is dangling a large set of keys. She smiles at me, revealing a gold front tooth.

"It is here," Dodo says.

I see that I had stopped very near to the bathroom. I feel a kind of lift that *I instinctively knew where to stop. Maybe my instincts are in place. Maybe everything will be all right.*

The old woman unlocks the door. She steps into the darkness, motions for me to follow. She pushes open another door. There's a little bit of light in here, coming from a small window. She unlocks a third door, and gestures for me to go in. I slip past her and step into a tiny water closet. Three walls press in tightly on a cracked, discolored toilet bowl. The smells of ammonia and rust seize my nose and throat, masking whatever other smells are there; nausea grips me. I start to close the door, but the old woman puts her hand against the frame and motions for me to keep it open. She points up at a broken light bulb, then to the outer room where the only light is coming from. She lets me know she will close the hallway door instead.

The door shuts. There is a loud swishing sound. It surprises me that the water is left to flush continuously, but I am glad for the sound; it drowns everything else out. I wonder if anyone would hear me if I screamed. I press my hand over my mouth and blow out hard several times. I open my coat and push down my tights. Gathering my coat above my waist, I bend over my thighs, keeping my butt in the air. I can feel the cold like a slap on my back. Tears are starting to stream down my face.

What is the matter with me? I have to pull myself together.

I try to concentrate on a black splotch on the floor that looks like some wild face. I can feel my own face crumbling, my body shaking. *How many minutes have passed? Will they come after me?*

I want the door completely shut. I want the darkness. I lean my head against the inner door and push until it clicks.

Everything will be all right, I tell myself. *The moment I've been waiting for has arrived. A miracle is about to happen.*

But what if it isn't a miracle? What if this is all a delusion, this idea that I want a child, that I can care for a child, that I will know how to mother a child? What experience do I have? Certainly none from my own un-mothered childhood. What if I'm just like her? What if I cannot love this child? Love enough?

I know it is not the baby I am afraid of, but myself. I'm afraid that somehow, I will miscarry again, that I will not be able to carry through, that I will want to run away.

A knock on the door jolts me back to earth.

"Corinne," Brian's voice comes muffled through the doors.

"Yes," I say. No, he can't hear that. I open the door a crack. "Yes," I repeat in a louder voice. "I'll be out in a minute."

I still have to pee.

I'm too tense. Maybe it can wait.

No, I have to go.

I can hear the rhythm of a prayer forming inside me. I don't seek the words, but they have come, ever since I was little, when I cannot pee.

Hail Mary, full of grace, the Lord is with thee. Blessed art thou among women and blessed is the fruit of thy womb, Jesus. Holy Mary, mother of God, pray for us sinners, now and at the hour of our death, amen.

Mary does not let me down; I suppress a giggle as a warm stream passes between my legs. I air-dry and pull up my tights. My hands feel like ice. I rub them together, slap my face.

"You okay?" Brian asks, back in the hallway.

"Yes," I say, as lightly as I can. I know he knows more, but he lets me be.

"Dodo is waiting for us."

I take his arm. "I'm glad you're here."

He looks at me, tenderly. "So am I," he says.

I'm feeling better now. A lightness, a buoyancy, almost a giddiness at the thought of the baby about to be delivered into my arms.

We catch up to Dodo who has stopped outside a door. Dodo smiles at me and pushes the door slowly open.

We are at the entrance of a small, airless room. What is that smell? It almost knocks me over. Against one wall, I see an iron crib, with a baby inside. The child is screaming, its face red and wet and contorted with rage. A nurse stands a few feet away, her back to the crib.

Doesn't she hear the crying? I look to Dodo.

"Is not your baby," she says. "A couple from Greece will take her."

A wave of relief passes through me—along with revulsion at my relief.

The nurse turns now, and sees us. She smiles broadly and steps aside. On a wooden table in front of her is another baby: tiny, anemic-looking, with swollen eyelids and doughy skin.

"This is your baby," Dodo says, smiling.

I take a few steps; then stop.

"Very good baby," I hear Dodo say.

"Good baby," the nurse echoes.

I know I'm supposed to be smiling and maybe I am, but everything inside me wants to flee. I cannot connect what is in front of me with the face in the photograph we were sent. That baby looked healthy and focused; this baby looks sick and puffy, its eyes vague, its body stiff.

Words spill out before I can catch them. "This is not the baby," I whisper.

I see alarm on Dodo's face. Brian looks at me in disbelief. This is the moment I have so feared—that I wanted to do anything to avoid.

But it's true, isn't it? They've switched babies on us. Something happened to the baby in the picture, and they're trying to substitute another baby.

The nurse, oblivious to the moment, is pulling off the infant's pajamas, her movements quick and efficient. It becomes clear where the foul smell is coming from. She unpins the gray cloth that serves as a diaper. Inside I see a huge mass of green mush. It looks like sick cow's manure. I feel myself gag. She throws the cloth into a metal pail.

She takes the naked baby to a sink against the wall, holds him under the faucet, and turns the tap on abruptly. The baby's body stiffens. A muted cry escapes my lips. I want to tell the nurse to be more gentle, to go more slowly. I'm amazed the baby doesn't scream at what must be ice-cold water. The nurse quickly pats him dry and without a pause in her movements, ties his bottom up with another gray cloth. Then she pulls the baby's arms and legs into a one-piece yellow-stained pajama. His eyes wander from person to person, a look of bewilderment on his face.

"Why you think this baby different?" Dodo asks, a slight edge in her voice.

What can I say? That he does not have red hair as they said? That he seems so tiny and pale and puffy? I cannot bear to hear the shallowness of my own thoughts, much less speak them. I am about to say something, when the nurse extends the baby toward me. Some involuntary reflex opens my arms.

He feels so light, so small. I didn't realize that babies could be this small. I look into his little face and the eyes that do not know where to land, and I can feel a sob rising in me.

The nurse motions toward an iron-framed bed against the wall. I sink into the worn mattress. The springs are sharp, but I don't mind; they're like an anchor. I hold the baby close against my body. I can feel his heat radiating through me.

Brian comes and stands behind me. "He's taking you in," he says.

Yes, the baby is looking up at me now.

"It's the same baby," Brian says. "Look at the eyes."

I take a breath. "Yes," I whisper.

"He's really looking at you," Brian repeats, almost in wonder.

I nod, my eyes filling up with tears. He's looking at me directly, steadily. He looks so calm and peaceful. I almost feel he's telling me—"It's me. I may look a little different from what you expected, but it's me. I've been waiting for you."

I feel limp. I can't believe this is actually happening to me. All I want is to hold this little creature in my arms and let him know that I am here for him. I feel his heart beating against my own. I see his little hands that were clenched a moment before, opening, the fingers reaching, like the fluttering of a baby bird.

* * *

The night is cool and wet. We walk several blocks along the main avenue. The street lamps aren't working. The only illumination is coming from the occasional passing car. There are some people walking and a few little groups huddled together. Brian and I speak softly so as not to draw attention.

"I can't believe I said this is not the baby," I say. "Dodo must have thought I was crazy."

"I'm sure she's heard worse," Brian says.

"Do you think the baby could tell that I pulled back?"

"I wouldn't worry about it. He liked you."

"You think so?"

"I know so. Look how he was glued to you at the end."

We walk on in silence, each wrapped in our own thoughts.

*   *   *

There's a call from Natasha when we get back to the hotel. Apparently, this is her second call.

"I told you it might be easier to speak to her from here," Brian whispers as I'm taking hold of the receiver.

"Don't go wandering at night," is the first thing she says.

"We're fine," I assure her. "It's not so bad here, really."

"Please!" she says, alarm in her voice. Then in a softer, different tone—"I heard you fell in love with the baby. I knew you would. But don't decide anything yet. Sleep on it. If you and Brian decide yes, you will need to give me a name right away. Don't worry, I'm on top of everything."

*   *   *

Up in our room, the electricity has suddenly gone off. Using my flashlight I go into the bathroom. I undress in the chilly air and with one of the towels give myself a cold sponge bath. I think of the baby as he held himself straight as an arrow under the faucet.

When I come out of the bathroom, Brian has already fallen asleep. I climb under the heavy bedspread that smells of age and camphor. I push the edge away from my face. I role over and try to sleep. My body is weary, but my brain does not want to rest. I keep seeing images of the baby in my arms. His little fingers . . . his large, dark, questioning eyes. I hope he couldn't feel my hesitancy. I hope he understood that it was just my own fear, nothing about him. He did seem to like me holding him. There was something so sweet and gentle and wise about him. I almost felt I was in the presence of an old soul. I worry that he didn't move his arms and legs more. He looked at us, watched us, but his body hardly moved. He also didn't show any interest in objects, not even the little stuffed dog we brought. I have to remember that this baby has not had much attention or stimulation. He may never have had a toy before. He's probably gone through so many hands. He hasn't had security. *He hasn't had a mother . . .*

*   *   *

January 11, 1997

We sleep till nearly ten o'clock, the ten-hour time difference taking its toll. In any case, the heavy drapes block the light, and, even when they're open, the barred windows and the gray day make it hard to know what time it is. There's no heat or water this morning.

An attractive woman enters the room carrying a pitcher of water. "I am sorry," she says. She introduces herself as "Galina, owner of house," and explains the man we met the other night was her husband, George. She hands me the pitcher and says, "We will bring you more water from store."

"Oh, don't worry," I say. "We can manage."

It's clear that water, heat, and electricity come and go. It's not really bothering us—we were prepared for much worse—but I can imagine how straining it must be as a way of life.

Galina is probably in her mid-thirties, and seems much younger than her husband. With her refined features, chiseled cheekbones, and large green eyes, she reminds me of Michelle Pfeiffer, "Georgian style." There is something genteel and elegant about her. When I compliment her on her home and on all the beautiful artwork, she tells us, "My husband is painter. All pictures in house are his."

As it turns out, they are also both actors—stars of the Rostoveli Theatre, the most important theater in Georgia.

"Is your theater performing now?" I ask.

"No, our theater is closed," Galina says with an air of resignation. "No money for theater. We hope soon will open."

She is interested to hear that Brian and I are also actors, but seems to take it in stride. I ask her if she's heard of the Actor's Studio. "Yes, of course," she says, and tells us that she and her husband performed in New York with their theater company (at the Brooklyn Academy of Music) during "better times."

*   *   *

Eke phones and says it is not possible to visit the baby today—"Hospital rules."

"How can that be?" I say. "We came all this way."

"I am sorry. Nothing can be done." She says she will come by later with the driver to show us some of Tbilisi.

To assuage my disappointment, I decide to take a walk while Brian stays at the house to study his lines. It's turned into a lovely day. The sun is out, and it almost feels warm. It's Saturday. People are strolling along the main avenue, Rosteveli Boulevard. It is reminiscent of the wide boulevards of Europe. Many of the buildings suggest an impressive past, with their large ornate arches and massive wooden doors. Still, the reminders of poverty and civil war abound, the beauty defaced by bullet holes, cracked pavement, crumbling bricks, and boarded-up doors and windows.

In contrast, the people look surprisingly well dressed. I had heard the Georgian women are beautiful, but the men, too, are quite striking with their dark, flashing looks. A few cafes are open, but most of the shops seem closed, and the ones that are open appear sparsely stocked. I see people shopping in open-air markets and kiosks.

I enter a park with a zoo and sit on a bench to watch the children as they look at the animals. The grounds and cages look neglected—in some places painfully so—but the animals don't appear to be starving. I see goats, sheep, a donkey, and even a llama. I think of the Central Park Zoo, with children screaming and tearing about with abandon on any given Saturday. Here, the children are amazingly well behaved.

People turn to stare at me—as if I'm the zoo's latest attraction. I don't think it's my face that intrigues them. With my brown hair and hazel eyes, I could pass for Georgian. I think it's my sneakers. No one here seems to wear sneakers, not even children.

Brian and I have been thinking about names for the baby. Thomas, David, Luke, Nicholas, Christopher. The nurses call him Kali. I like that. Kalipkul is a beautiful name, though it might be a difficult name to carry in the States.

Sitting on the bench, I suddenly remember a dream I had last night. I dreamed that Al Jolson was Georgian. Al Jolson? Haven't thought of him in a long time. When I was a little girl and home, sick with the flu, I saw *The Jolson Story* on the *Million Dollar Movie* on television, starring Larry Parks. The movie repeated over and over during the week, and I couldn't get enough of it. I completely fell in love with Jolson and his music. I learned all of his songs and endlessly sang them and tap-danced, to the delight of our Jamaican housekeeper, Birdie, who especially liked my "Mammy" and "Sonny Boy." Is the dream telling me the baby will be a future entertainer? Or . . . is it trying to tell me this baby is *the one*—my Sonny Boy?

*   *   *

Later from the car, Eke points out the Philharmonia, the Opera House, and the Rosteveli Theater.

"Are there concerts going on?" Brian asks.

"Yes," she says, "but not so much now."

As we drive through the center of town, we pass a university. "We have many universities in Tbilisi," Eke tells us, "but no money for books." She speaks of the high price Georgia has had to pay in exchange for freedom. She doesn't hide her hatred of Communism. "My grandfather was university professor. Stalin's men killed him."

We pass Republic Square, formerly Stalin Square, and go up a winding wooded drive to the Television Broadcast Station, atop a hill overlooking the city. The side of the building is riddled with bullet holes. We continue into the old section of town. We stop by Sioni Cathedral, the most famous church in Georgia, dating back to the fifth century. Eke tells us that during Communist times it was forbidden to go to church, and that the church was only recently reopened.

Then we drive further outside the city. In the distance, we see an ancient-looking stone tower, which we learn is a monastery, dating back to the eleventh century. We turn off the highway and head up the mountain. We park the car and hike up the hill. The wind is fierce and nearly blows us over. At the top of the promontory is a sweeping view of Tbilisi, the Mtkvari River, and the surrounding mountain range. It's a majestic and breathtaking sight, and suggests a past of romance and legend. This is how I pictured Georgia in my imagination—a land of high mountains and ancient civilization, land of the Golden Fleece. As we near the entrance of the church, a small, strange-looking boy in a worn monk's cloak and a face that could be out of the Middle Ages silently signals us to put our cameras away before we enter. It's cold and stark inside, with no place to sit, but also beautiful in its bareness, with stone walls and a large fresco of Saint Nino, the patron saint of Georgia, who introduced Christianity to the country in the fourth century. When we get outside the church, Eke begins to tell us Nino's story:

"Long ago, in ancient times, in our land there were only barbarians, but there was a woman, named Nino, who was devoted to Jesus and had saved a dying child by holding the child in her arms and praying. News of this spread through the kingdom. Then the queen became sick and no one could cure her. She heard about Nino and sent for her. Nino held the queen in her arms and prayed in the name of Jesus, and the queen was cured. The king was so happy. He offered Nino precious gifts, but Nino refused. She said she had given her life to Christ and lived on prayer, the way others lived on food. Then one night, it was very dark and the king became lost in the woods. He was very afraid, and all alone. The king prayed to Nino's Christ, and in that same moment, the sun came up, and the king was saved. The king was so happy, and he went again to Nino and asked how he could repay her. Nino told him, 'Build a church.' The king followed Nino's wishes, and this is how Christianity was brought to our land."

On the way back to our hotel, we pick up our pictures from the film store. Oddly, there seems to be a Kodak store on every other block. I wonder who is taking all these pictures?

In some of the shots, the baby appears quite focused and perfectly fine, but in others, he looks disturbingly dazed and swollen. It occurs to me that we might find a pediatrician who could look at the pictures.

Galina is out, but George, with the assistance of his two nieces who speak some English, makes several calls for us, and we make an appointment to see a doctor in the morning.

*   *   *

January 12, 1997

From the war-damaged exterior and stairwell, the doctor's building could appear to be a tenement house in a slum, but within his apartment, it is lovely and speaks of art and music. Beautiful antique furniture, Impressionist-style paintings (painted, we are told, by the doctor's uncle), shelves and shelves of books, a piano, a guitar, and various other string instruments fill the apartment.

The kindly faced pediatrician leads us into his study. This room, too, is overflowing with books and papers. The doctor's daughter, a bubbly eighteen-year-old, serves as our interpreter. I'm amazed at how many of the young people here speak English.

Dr. Uberi looks at the photos. He smiles immediately. After a few moments, he turns to his daughter and speaks.

"My father says the baby has very good face," the young woman says eagerly. She makes a gesture to indicate good proportions. "But he will go with you to see baby and make sure everything is fine."

"Oh, I don't know if that would be possible," Brian quickly says. "I mean we would love it, but it could cause trouble and jeopardize our situation."

"It might seem as though an outside person were coming to investigate," I explain. "It might be taken as a message that maybe we doubt what they say is true."

The young woman communicates our words of concern.

The doctor smiles and shakes his head.

"My father says is not a problem," the young woman tells us. "He says all the doctors are his friends. He says he can go to hospital alone."

"Maybe it would be good," I whisper to Brian.

"My father says to not worry," the daughter says, with great assurance. "He will tell you truth."

When we ask Dr. Uberi if the baby looks more Georgian or Azerbaijani, he says, "Georgian." Then he laughs good-naturedly and says, "Azerbaijanis are a good people, too."

"My father says name Kalipkul is a noble name," the daughter tells us.

The doctor's manner is warm and expansive. It feels comforting just to be with him.

*   *   *

We go see the baby right after seeing the doctor. Eke is home, sick with a toothache and Zauri, our driver, takes us. Upon entering the hospital, the first thing we see is a lamb. It is at the end of the hallway, drinking from a metal pail. A beam of light from above casts a hazy aura around him. It is a mystical image.

"*That's a first,*" Brian says.

"Maybe it's a good omen," I say.

Today my reaction to the baby is totally different. Released from my fear, he looks *so beautiful.* Immediately, he fastens his eyes on me. He's three months old today. I've brought another toy, a multicolored sock with a little bell on it. But he doesn't want it. In fact, he starts to cry and continues to cry until I put the sock away.

He seems to prefer eyes looking at him, and arms holding him.

The puffiness around his eyes has gone down, and he's not sneezing as much. We're again amazed at how he doesn't make a sound when the nurse holds him under the cold running water to wash his tush. He keeps his body straight as though flying in the air and just looks at us.

We stay with him for an hour and a half, all the time we're allowed. By the end, we feel completely decided that he is ours. Brian and I both want to get the process moving right away. Eke seemed to imply yesterday that everyone in the agency is nervous about certain laws that could be changing.

* * *

In search of a cup of coffee I leave Brian to work on his part, and walk down Rosteveli Boulevard. It's about 6 p.m. and nearly dark. I find a dimly lit luncheonette with an all-glass storefront that seems to be open. I go in. There's a young man and woman sitting at a table in a haze of smoke. It takes a moment to communicate *coffee* to the man behind the counter. Somehow it doesn't seem like an ordinary thing to order, but then he smiles and brings out a jar of Nescafe. I nod gratefully.

I take a seat by the window, away from the smoke. I hope the young couple won't think me anti-social, but they seem pretty wrapped up in each other, and probably appreciate the space.

The coffee is lukewarm, but better than nothing. I take the pictures of the baby from my coat pocket. As I look at them, I'm having this surreal feeling that my whole life is being re-formulated in some alchemical mixing bowl. Perhaps I've died and just don't know it and I'm already in another life. And here I am, sitting in a dark café on a street in Tblisi, Georgia, looking at pictures of a baby who is about to become my son. How did I get here? How did this happen?

* * *

January 13, 1997

"Yes! We're sure we want to adopt him," we say to Dodo over the phone the next morning.

We hound her with questions: "How long will it take?" "What else do we need to do?" "When is the soonest we can get him home?"

Surely, it can be faster than the six to eight weeks that Natasha talked about, I think. I say to Dodo, "You said it could possibly finish very fast."

"Yes, when government gives permission," she replies, a sigh in her voice.

For all our enthusiasm, her answers remain the same: nothing can be done for the next two weeks, not until the twenty-fifth. But then she abruptly says with more energy, "I will go to ministry tomorrow and see."

*　　*　　*

At the hospital, I am amazed at how much can change in three days. My first reaction to the baby was to pull back; now I'm in love!

Brian is totally committed. I've never seen such a change in a person. A week ago, he was willing to leave the whole thing up to me. Now I think there is nothing he wouldn't do for this baby. It's incredible how much the baby has changed, too. He's so much more alive and responsive today than he was on our first visit. He's even waving his arms and legs. He cries when I put him down in his bed and quiets as soon as he's back in my arms.

He knows me now. Knows us. It's astonishing! He still hasn't fully smiled, but the beginnings are there. He's even starting to take in the stuffed Dalmatian. He seems to like it now when the little dog is placed by his side.

We try out our list of names on him. Christopher Kali is what he seems to like best. We say it over and over again. He looks at us so open and trusting. How to let him know that we will be back very soon?

A burst of voices pierces the moment as Dr. Uberi enters, followed by several of the hospital staff. We were afraid this might happen. The large woman with the disgruntled features whom we've seen in the administrative office looks on distrustfully, as Dr. Uberi checks the baby's head and reflexes. He smiles to us and gives an affirmative thumbs-up, but I have the feeling he is being prevented from doing a more thorough examination.

*　　*　　*

"*Why you do such things without asking?*" Dodo says sternly when we're in the car. She sounds very offended.

"The doctor is a friend of the people we're staying with," I say, trying to be as casual about it as possible.

"*They are actors,*" she says. "They don't know about such things."

"We were told that the baby was two months premature and that he was very sick when he arrived at the hospital," Brian says.

"Who told you that?" Dodo asks, looking at us from her rearview mirror.

"A doctor at the hospital yesterday," I say.

"They gave you 'official' report," Dodo counters.

Brian and I look to each other. Natasha had warned us that they have to exaggerate the baby's physiological and psychological ailments in order for it to be eligible for foreign adoption. We don't say anything further. We ride in silence for a while. I hope this isn't going to cause any trouble. I know it's important to Dodo that we believe what she says is true, and I do feel she genuinely cares about the baby. Still, I don't regret that we went to see Dr. Uberi.

Now, in a more supportive tone, Dodo says that we should try to get our senator or congressman to write to the Georgian government asking to release the baby.

"You tell them you have accepted child, you love him and will provide him the best."

She lets us know that Senator Kennedy helped get a baby released not so long ago.

"They can't refuse the Americans," she says. "They help us so much."

She goes on to say that she will not be able to keep the baby at the hospital much longer. "Maybe two more weeks," she says. "Government says we can only keep baby in hospital if he is sick. If he is healthy, he must go to orphanage."

I feel a squeeze in my chest. "But why can't you keep him?" I appeal. "He was premature."

"He is normal weight now," Dodo says, with a sigh. "I try as long as possible, but I am afraid in two weeks, they will say he must go."

She drops us off at the hotel. "I will come in evening and we will talk more," she says.

*   *   *

This is our last day. We leave early tomorrow morning.

How to get Kali out quickly? Staying in a hospital is not the best of situations, but at least the nurses there seem to care about him, and he's being fed regularly. Eke tells us the orphanage is terrible and that everything there will be much more restricted—food, heat—and mostly, the needed attention and affection.

Up in our room I say to Brian, "If they're having this meeting in ten days, maybe I should just stay here. Maybe being here could speed things up, and that way I could continue to be with the baby until they finish the paperwork. And then, I could bring the baby home myself."

"It would be great if they would let you," Brian says.

"Why wouldn't they let me? We're paying for the hotel. I'm sure the actors would appreciate the extra money. I'll just have to contact the New School and let them know."

*   *   *

In the evening Dodo phones us. She sounds depressed. She says she is unable to come see us because her daughter (age three, adopted) isn't feeling well.

I tell Dodo my idea of staying here until the twenty-fifth.

"I am sorry," she says, "this is *not* possible. We have no permission for such things. Hospital has strict rules."

"Could we get permission?" I ask.

"No one can give such thing."

"What about Natasha asking?"

"Is not so easy. She must be careful."

Dodo then says that the baby's "personal" pediatrician (the dark-haired doctor we met the first day) will come to see us tonight. I have the uncomfortable feeling that besides whatever else is going on with her daughter, Dodo isn't coming herself because she doesn't know what else to say to us. It's becoming more and more evident that she and everyone involved with the agency is very worried that the whole adoption process could be stopped.

*   *   *

The hospital pediatrician arrives, along with Eke to translate. Eke has the tired, strained look of when we first saw her at the airport. We sit downstairs, in the salon—she and Eke on the brocade couch, Brian and I in the two velvet armchairs opposite the couch. As it was the first day, the doctor's manner is strangely cool. She barely looks at us, and directs her answers to Eke.

Eke tells us the doctor would like to straighten out any misunderstanding we might have about the baby's medical record.

"Doctor says baby was definitely only three weeks premature. He did need oxygen at birth because cord was around his neck, but he was all right. Doctor says mother's water was 'dirty.' She says most of the babies who come to them have 'dirty water.'"

I want to ask what 'dirty water' means, but Eke goes on.

"Doctor says that baby was sick when he came to them, but that he was better very fast and that he is normal for his age." Though now in the next sentence, Eke says that because the baby was premature, his behavior is more that of an infant of nine weeks than twelve weeks.

Brian brings out the photos of the baby. For the first time the doctor's face relaxes into a smile, revealing an unexpected softness. It's been hard to understand her coldness, but now I can see that she does seem to be genuinely fond of Kali. The atmosphere warms up. She even looks at us now. I think she knows we really love him.

"Doctor says the baby needs massage," Eke continues. "She says because of asphyxiation, there's tension in the body."

Brian and I nod. "Is there any possibility of the baby getting massage here, until we can get him out?" Brian asks.

"Doctor says she will see if it is possible," Eke says.

I say, "Please tell her that the baby's body has loosened up quite a bit since we've been here. It's almost been miraculous the change in three days."

Eke translates. The doctor smiles again.

"Doctor says that when baby will be with you and have your love and care, he will be completely normal child."

I'm feeling so grateful that the doctor came to see us. When she leaves she shakes our hand and wishes us the best.

*   *   *

It is Georgian New Year's Eve, though we would never know it had we not been told. Nothing much seems to be going on in the streets. The owners have a few guests over, but it's a quiet party. They've invited us to join them, but we need to pack, and besides, we're not in much of a party mood. A bonding has begun with Kali. He trusts us. Will our leaving be felt as another abandonment?

"We have to get this kid out," Brian says. "No matter what."

With heavy hearts, we go upstairs to pack. A car will come to take us to the airport at 4:30 a.m. We arrived in the dark and we'll be leaving in the dark. Why can't we just take him?

*   *   *

At the airport in Istanbul, I see a sign for a flight to Tel Aviv.

"I think I should go to Israel," I say to Brian. "I wanted to see Colette and show her the baby's picture, and this way, if things open, up I can get back to Georgia the same day—in a few hours practically."

"Then do it," Brian says. "I'll start sending out letters right away."

We go to the check-in counter and I change my ticket. There is just enough time to catch the next flight to Tel Aviv. We hurry to the gate. We hold each other close as strangers rush about us, each with their own life, their own destiny.

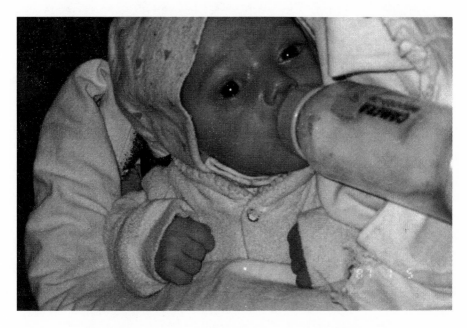

The photo we were waiting for. Cali at two months old.

As soon as I held him in my arms, there was a special connection between us.

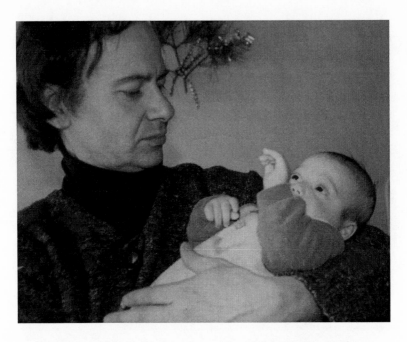

Brian and Cali the first day at the Children's Hospital.

Cali meets "Georgie"

The monastery

View from the monastery overlooking the Mtkvari River valley

Street market in Tbilisi near Chavchavadzis Avenue.

Women from the countryside prepare their vegetables for the market.

Israel

January 14, 1997

My suitcase does not land with me in Tel Aviv. It seems it's still in Georgia. Turkish Airlines says they will deliver it as soon as it arrives.

After a long bus ride to Jerusalem, a cab ride that takes me to the wrong hotel, then another cab ride, I finally arrive at the Jerusalem Tower Hotel. From my room, I can see the Old City. Colette must live somewhere nearby, I think

I buy a few necessities, a toothbrush, toothpaste, shampoo, a nightgown, underpants, and then set off to find Colette. I show the hotel concierge the address, and he tells me I will need to take a taxi. I politely thank him, and confidently set off on foot.

Two hours later, I am still trying to find her street. Each time I ask for directions, I am told, "Too far, too far, take a taxi." Finally, with night approaching and the neighborhood increasingly desolate, I hail down the one taxi that passes.

"Shimone twenty-eight," I tell the driver. At first, he seems not to know the street, but then gruffly says, "Okay, okay."

"Catacomb," I say. "I think it's straight. That's what I was told."

"I know where it is," he barks in a heavy, middle-eastern accent. I have no idea if the man is a Jew or a Palestinian. He has a Semitic face, but beyond that, I can't tell. He slams his foot down on the accelerator and then makes a sharp U-turn. He drives extremely fast and does not put on the meter.

"Sir," I say, "I think it's the other way."

"I know where it is," he shouts, "Shimone Street."

For the first time since leaving New York, I really feel in danger for my life. I imagine myself screaming, throwing myself out of the cab, my body in pieces on the pavement. But I can't die now, I tell myself, I have a baby to adopt.

"I don't think you put the meter on," I say, making one last attempt.

He doesn't answer.

I sit back in the seat. There is nothing to do but pray.

Strangely, I make it. The driver only charges me five dollars and is almost friendly as he says goodbye.

I press the buzzer on the blue door that is marked 28.

I wait . . . "Yes," a voice says over the intercom. I suspect it must be her. I tell her I'm from New York and a friend of Viviane Lind and Catherine Segonzac. "Catherine suggested I . . ."

"Oh, it is too late for me," the voice interrupts in a refined French-sounding accent. "Come back tomorrow at 4:30."

"Oh . . . okay," I say.

"Shalom," she says.

" . . . Shalom."

I turn to go. Night has suddenly fallen. I hurry to find a cab.

*   *   *

January 15, 1997

I have a few hours before my meeting with Colette, so I decide to walk to the Old City. I enter the Jaffa gate and am soon blasted with a potpourri of exotic colors, scents, and sounds, coming from all the outdoor shops and bazaars. I lose myself in the winding narrow streets. I walk the Via Doloroso, the path Jesus took on his last day before the crucifixion. I visit the Church of the Holy Sepulcher said to be the site where Jesus was buried. I visit the hall where the Last Supper took place, King David's Tomb, Mount Zion, the Wailing Wall, and the Dome of the Rock. I walk and walk through the streets thousands of years old. The sense of sacredness and religious devotion emanating from these ancient stones is painfully at odds with the palpable atmosphere of tension and unrest.

I find myself looking up at a building and see inscribed in the stone surface *"Saving One Child Is Like Saving the World."*

Thoughts of Kali swirl in my mind. Has he noticed our absence? Does he understand that we are coming back?

* * *

At 4:30, I am on Colette's doorstep again.

"Come in," she says over the intercom.

The door is ajar. I make my way through a dark, narrow hallway, passing two tiny, compactly filled rooms, and arrive in a third, larger room. A lamp at the far end of the room illuminates an elderly woman in a pleated skirt and red cardigan, stretched out on a divan, surrounded with colorful pillows.

"Come," Colette says with a slow wave of her hand. Somehow I was expecting a heavier, perhaps more eccentric-looking character. Catherine once told me that Colette had rarely been out of her apartment in thirty years. But the handsome, elegant-looking woman I see before me, with white hair meticulously pulled back in a bun and full, carefully painted red lips, strikes me as anything but reclusive.

I present her with a box of chocolates. I had wanted to bring flowers, but the one flower shop I saw along the way was closed.

"Thank you. That is very kind of you," she says. "I am so sorry that I could not receive you last night. I was very tired. Now I must speak softly to preserve my voice."

I notice a repeated flutter in her left eye. I wonder if it is a tick, or a momentary ailment.

Her English is very good. I was expecting to speak to her in French, since Catherine had told me that Colette was originally from Algeria—from a very old line of Sephardic Cabalistic teachers. "Masters," Catherine had said.

I also expected a grander apartment. I was told she never charged for her classes, and so I presumed her to be wealthy. I can see that she has many old and beautiful art pieces, but the apartment itself is small and modest.

Colette asks me about myself. I explain that I'm an actress and teacher, and have just arrived from the Republic of Georgia, where I am hoping to adopt a baby. I reach for the pictures of Kali. Colette glances at them and says, "Didn't Catherine tell you that I have not done morphology since 1984?"

I feel a huge wave of disappointment.

"You can only tell with a baby the first week," she continues. "After that, the face changes too much. Every day it changes."

She looks again at the pictures. "I see he is intelligent. He has a good forehead, good ears . . . Georgians are a strong people."

"Why do you want to adopt?" she asks abruptly.

Her directness jolts me. I suddenly feel put on the spot, and for a moment find myself at a loss for words.

" . . . It just came about that way," I say, not really wanting to get into anything more.

"How old are you?" she asks.

I can feel my face flushing. My actress's vanity makes me hesitate. I wonder if she's going to tell me that I'm too old? "Fortyeee . . ."

"You look twenty-five!" she cuts me off, freeing me from my misery. She sits up from her reclined position with surprising vigor. "I am very interested in adoption. I have a friend who adopted from Brazil. It has been very good. When I was a child, I imagined for a while that I was adopted. Don't worry about the child being premature. I was a month premature, and see, I am eighty-eight now. I was also born with a heart defect, as was my brother. The doctor said we would not live beyond twenty, and we are both alive today, and my brother is a genius." She pauses for a moment and then adds, "Being told that I would die taught me to live each day as though it were my last."

With the mention of Brazil, I bring up my grandmother whom Colette is strongly reminding me of, in her aristocratic manner and air of authority. "She lived in Rio," I say. "I went to Brazil many times to see her."

"She was Brazilian?" Colette asks.

"No. Polish," I say. "She went there as a refugee during the war."

"Jewish?" Colette asks.

"In the background, yes, though she was brought up Catholic, and so was my mother. She came from a wealthy, upper-class family in Warsaw. She lost everything during the war . . . and then started over again in Brazil. She had a difficult life, but managed to live to ninety-five."

"A difficult life makes you stronger," Colette says. "I had a very difficult life, but up till now, I have succeeded in everything I have done. I had many obstacles from outside, but I succeeded."

In the two hours that I spend with Colette, she tells me many stories about her childhood and her life and the challenges she faced. I ask the secret to her success.

"Not caring about success," she says. "Doing what I have to do *well*. My success is a *periphenomenon*. Do you know what that means? A phenomenon coming as the result of another phenomenon."

With some effort, she gets up from the divan. I move to assist her, but she gestures that she can manage. "I am fine," she says. "It is only my legs. One is shorter than the other from an accident I had four years ago. It makes it painful for me to walk."

She makes her way into an adjoining room and returns carrying a large ancient-looking paper, covered in writing. She tells me that it's a chart mapping her family lineage that shows that she's a direct descendant to King David. She says that in keeping with her heritage, she has had a duty in this life to do the best for herself and for others. "A day without intention is a wasted day," she says.

Somehow, the hours with Colette fill a hunger in me—for wisdom, for guidance, for wanting to lead a conscious, purposeful life—more important even than showing her the pictures of Kali. By the end of our time together, I feel more grounded and hopeful, and, interestingly, more trusting of my *own* intuition.

As I'm about to leave, she looks at me with a face full of kindness and knowing. "I am teaching a class on Monday. You are welcome to come. It is good to be alone at times, but then we must come together with others. We must share with others—otherwise, what we receive in being alone is lost. We are here to share who we are and what we have."

* * *

I enter my hotel room just in time to answer the phone. It's Brian.

"I fell asleep halfway through rehearsal, but they said I did great. I don't know if they were trying to make me feel good, or boost their own morale. Anyway, they loved the pictures of the baby. I've been showing them to everyone."

I can hear the pride in his voice as he says this.

"I've been doing the same," I say. I tell him of my visit to Colette.

"Sounds like your trip to Israel has already been worth it," he says.

"Any news from Natasha?" I ask.

"It's back to the usual. She says she hasn't been able to get through to Dodo."

"Did you tell her that I could go right back to Georgia from here?"

"I did, but it's looking pretty complicated . . . I called Kennedy's office, but I know I'll have to get to him directly. Joe, the older man I hired at work, thinks I should contact this congressman from Rockland County, but I've never even heard of him. I don't think he could do much. I'm going to focus on Kennedy."

Sitting on my hotel bed, I look again at the pictures: the one of Kali snuggled in my arms and the one of Brian holding Kali.

I think back to the time I first met Brian. I was at the Actor's Studio working on a one-act comedy, *Laundry and Bourbon*, with Sally Kirkland and my friend, Frances Fisher. The scene went well and afterward, a sensitive-looking guy with longish dark hair approached me, smiling shyly. "I liked your work," he said.

I remember thinking that there was something familiar about him.

"I was your husband, you know."

"Oh?" I replied, "And when was that? Did I miss something?"

"In *Lone Star*," he said, a twinkle in his eye, "I played Cletis. Your husband."

Lone Star was the companion piece to *Laundry and Bourbon*, both written by James McClure. Brian told me that he had performed it in Los Angeles and played my character's husband. As it turned out, we had both been in LA around the same time, and studied with the same teacher, Peggy Feury.

"Maybe we passed each other in the night," Brian said.

A month later, I was at a sweat lodge in upstate New York with Frances. It was her birthday, May 11th. It was also my father's birthday. He had died three years before from lung cancer. A small group sat in a circle around red-hot coals in a steaming tent with an Indian chief who was conducting a purification ceremony. My prayer was to make peace with my father's death and with the grief I felt at losing him.

It happened that Jo Anderson, another actress from the Actor's Studio was also partaking in the sweat. I didn't know her very well, but as we were walking out, she mentioned that she was working with a director named Brian Hickey. My ears pricked up.

"Do you like working with him?" I asked.

"Oh yes, he's great," Jo said. I remember feeling a burst of excitement at hearing this. That fall, I saw their piece at the Studio and loved it. It was so simple and honest. On impulse, I got Brian's phone number and called him. I wasn't aware of any romantic interest at that point, only that I was attracted to his talent. We agreed to meet that night to discuss the possibility of working on something together.

"Would Grand Central be okay?" I asked. "I have a train to catch at 8:05. We could meet at 7:00 in the little coffee shop next to the main entrance on Forty-second."

"Sure," he said.

He didn't show at seven, or at eight. At 8:20, I saw him sauntering up. I remember thinking—"he's almost an hour and a half late. Why is he walking so casually?"

"Oh, I'm sorry," he said sincerely, when he caught sight of me. "I thought you meant the Lexington Avenue entrance."

I don't like it when people are late, and I don't really know what made me wait that day and miss my train—but I did. We went into the coffee shop, and talked, and I missed the next train as well. After we began seeing one another, he would tell me that one of the things that first made him love me was the fact that I had *waited*. It was ironic that he was drawn to me for a quality that I do not possess—patience.

As I look now at the picture of Brian smiling at the baby, I realize that our first meeting at Grand Central was October 12th—exactly ten years before Kali was born.

We three should be *together* instead of on three separate continents.

*   *   *

January 17, 1997

My suitcase arrives, and just in time. It's gotten cold and rainy.

With a break in the clouds, I take up a young Palestinian's offer to show me the Old City. I had seen him the other day at the entrance of the Jaffa gate and felt drawn to his intelligent, refined face.

He shows me many of the same sites I had seen Wednesday morning, but today there are far more soldiers in the Old City. "It is because it is Friday, the day when all Palestinians go to pray in the Mosque," my young guide tells me. "And it is Ramadan."

It is also the Jewish Sabbath and there are many soldiers guarding the West Wall. It's so strange that a *holy day*—a day reserved for prayer—should bring out the guns. A woman at the hotel this morning told me that many Israelis will not even go into the Old City. "It's too dangerous," she said. "A whole generation of children have not seen it."

*   *   *

I sit by the window and watch the sheets of rain coming down. I wait till after midnight and call Brian in New York.

"Are you up?"

"I am *now*," he mumbles. "What time is it?"

"It must be close to 7:30 your time. You need to sleep some more?"

"No, no."

"How's the play going?"

"We open tonight," he says. "Money people are coming. It's crazy. We're not ready. I don't even know all my lines."

"Maybe the play will do better that way," I offer.

"Tell that to the playwright," Brian says.

There's a pause.

"I called the State Department about the baby," he goes on, in a more awake, but somber tone. "They said they can't interfere in the affairs of a sovereign nation, but when we get the baby out—to send them a picture. Can you believe that? Anyway, I sent a letter to Kennedy explaining everything, with pictures of you and the baby, and I mentioned my past connections to his brother's campaign when I was in college, and that I was a state officer in the Young Democrats. Hopefully, that'll help get his attention. I also wrote to Jimmy Carter. This seems like the perfect kind of thing for him. I wrote a letter to Shevardnadze, too. I want to fax it, but Natasha says that she has to do it. She says that if it got out that she gave me his fax number, she could lose all her Georgian contacts. I got so pissed at her. I was really blunt. I told her that this letter better get off right away. She says casually, 'Oh, he'll come out . . . and if this doesn't work, we'll get you another baby.' As if one baby can replace another. If that baby goes to an orphanage, I don't know what I'll do."

I'm struck by Brian's intensity.

"Don't think about it anymore today," I say. "You have an opening to focus on. I know you will be great."

I feel guilty. Brian is doing so much, and what am I doing to help? Is my stay here accomplishing anything? It doesn't sound as though things are going to clear up enough for me to go back to Georgia in the next few days.

But I know I couldn't have gone right back to New York after seeing the baby. I couldn't go back to "life as usual." I needed this time to clear and to cleanse—to make space for the "new life" that is to come. Somehow I knew this. My soul knew this when the thought of this trip first came about. I had never had much interest in going to Israel before, and then, suddenly, it became a burning desire. Not Israel as much as Jerusalem. And maybe not Jerusalem of today, as much as the Jerusalem of all time.

*   *   *

January 20, 1997

I go to Colette's class. There are about twelve people, mostly women, all in the healing professions. The class is entitled "Images, Language of the Inside." Colette looks regal as she sits in a high-backed chair.

Over the next hour and a half, Colette gives a series of exercises. With each one we are to close our eyes, breathe out three times counting down from three to one, and then allow for whatever image spontaneously appears. In one visualization, I see a bridge arching over the two sides of my brain. Then I see another bridge, extending from the center of this first bridge up into the heavens. I can feel this *vertical* bridge pulling up the horizontal bridge, taking me along with it. For a moment, it's as if I disappear into the ethers. I then reemerge and descend back to earth. The next thing I see is a snail, which then becomes a scarab.

I tell Colette the experience.

"The snail cannot protect itself, but the scarab can," she says. "The scarab is able to push a weight much heavier than itself, and for that it is a symbol for being able to do the *impossible*."

In another exercise, I have the image of a very large tree with the lower branches growing down into the ground and the upper branches curving toward the sky. Then the branches of the upper part come together in a circle, and the branches of the lower part form a circle . . . creating a kind of figure eight for the whole. Then I see a baby lying horizontally between the two circles.

*   *   *

After the class, I feel the need to walk and reflect. I follow the long dusty road all the way up to the Mount of Olives and visit the Garden of Gethsemane. The gnarled olive trees are over a thousand years old. I think how much these trees have witnessed.

Tomorrow they are supposed to meet to clear up the adoption regulations in Georgia. I'm still hanging on to the slim hope that Brian will receive positive news.

On the way back to the Old City, I come upon a cave. Lanterns of all colors hang from the ceiling. I feel drawn to enter. A solemn-looking Orthodox priest hands me a candle and points to some steps. "Tomb of Mary," he says.

I take the steps down. I stay a long while, in the silence, in the darkness, free from guides and tourists.

"Help me, Mother of all Mothers. Guide me to this little one."

*   *   *

Brian calls at midnight. "It's not going to work to go back to Georgia."

Obstacles

January 26, 1997

The towering New York City skyline looks awesome to me as our plane descends through a crystal blue sky. It feels as though I've been away a very long time.

I go as fast as I can through customs and baggage claim and then look for Brian. When I don't see him, I assume he must be doing a matinee.

I take a cab to the city. Myshkin and Frenchie lavish me with kisses. They're all fluffy and sweet smelling. Brian must have washed them specially this morning.

An hour passes when the phone rings. It's Brian. "You'll never guess where I am," he says.

My heart skips a beat. "Georgia?" I say.

He laughs. "The airport."

"Oh no."

"I wanted to surprise you. The play was canceled today because of the Super Bowl. I'll be home as soon as I can.

*   *   *

The day is clear, but the temperature well below freezing. Brian and I rush into the corner diner and snuggle into a booth that looks out onto Seventy-second Street. A familiar waiter greets us and brings us two cups of coffee.

"The U.S. State Department is calling it a *moratorium*," Brian says.

"A moratorium? What does that mean again, exactly?"

"It means that all international adoptions in Georgia are on hold and no new ones can be initiated. It's official government policy, by decree. The only way around it is to get an exception granted by the president."

Brian shows me the letter he wrote to Shevardnadze.

Dear President Shevardnadze,

We are in the middle of the process of adopting an infant child in the Republic of Georgia. The child was born October 12, 1996, premature, underweight and suffered from asphyxiation due to a wrapped umbilical cord. The mother is a single woman of Azerbaijani extraction, and relinquished the baby at birth.

After having been told about the child, we flew to Tbilisi to see him and to finalize the adoption process. The child was at first extremely quiet, almost sad looking, but he couldn't take his eyes off of my wife. Little by little, he began to come to life, and really bond with my wife. The nurses there say that once these infants meet their adoptive parents, they usually gain an average of a pound a week. As this tiny child's eyes lit up when we held him in our arms, it was clear to the nurses and everyone around that he was already looking to us as his parents. And we, likewise, had completely fallen in love with him.

As we attempted to finalize the papers, we were told that the moratorium had just been announced. I'm sure you can imagine our shock and horror.

The child is currently at the Republic Children's Hospital in Tbilisi where the nurses there are giving him good care. In two weeks, however, if we are not allowed to adopt Kalipkul, he will be sent to the orphanage. He has already been shuttled to two institutions. He is still suffering from the physical and neurological symptoms of asphyxiation, and, of course, from having been abandoned. He is a very sweet, delicate child. He desperately needs the continued bonding of a loving mother and father.

We beg your assistance in permitting us to complete the adoption process and give this baby a loving home. If you can find it in your heart to help us, we will be eternally grateful. Even though the child's birth mother was not an ethnic Georgian, we will pledge to bring this baby up with a full pride and understanding of his birth land. We found the Georgian people to be extremely kind, open and generous of spirit, and the country beautiful.

President Shevardnadze, we thank you from the bottom of our hearts for giving this your consideration, and pray that you will understand our plight and allow us to give this boy a home.

I can feel my eyes filling up with tears. I reach over the table and place my hand over Brian's. He smiles, almost shyly, and then tenderly places his free hand over mine. A4s we hold each other's gaze, I think how I'm discovering a side of my husband I never knew before. He was always somewhat detached about the idea of having a baby. It wasn't a desperate need for him; it wasn't something he had to have, until . . . he saw *this* baby.

The waiter pours us a refill.

"I told you I wrote to Jimmy Carter and to Walter Posner, the Russian newsman I met last year," Brian says. "Posner called me back from Moscow. He says that he's coming to New York soon. He says he knows Shevardnadze. Maybe he can help. Also, the minister of tourism from Georgia is coming to Washington this week. We should try to contact him."

"What does Natasha say about what's happening?" I ask.

"She says that we shouldn't get our hopes up. She says letters have been written before on behalf of babies and that they didn't help. I told her that wasn't true. I told her I know a letter from Ted Kennedy helped release a child. She said that was an exception. 'That's what we want, I told her, an exception.' I just get the feeling she's scared to do anything. But Dodo has been wonderful. She said she was able to get a twenty-five-day extension on the baby's stay in the hospital."

*   *   *

Though I've been up over twenty-four hours, I'm too wired to sleep. Brian and I talk late into the night and watch the videotape we took in Georgia. I see how I so overreacted that first day. I worried that the baby looked sick and that he wasn't moving enough. Now I can see he was moving plenty. He looks so beautiful to me!

Hopefully, we will be going back to Georgia very soon. Which reminds me—I have to teach tomorrow.

*   *   *

January 27, 1997

Terrible news! They've taken the baby to the orphanage. While I was at school, Brian spoke with Dodo on the phone and she said that the chief doctor would not allow the baby to stay in the hospital any longer.

"But what about the twenty-five days?" I ask.

"She says it's because the baby isn't sick anymore," Brian says. "So then I called Natasha. She tells me that Dodo doesn't want us calling her in Georgia. She says that Dodo is angry about it. I tell her that it was Dodo who gave us her number, who said for us to call, and it was Dodo who told us to fax President Shevardnadze. She says, 'You have to understand Georgians. They don't know how to say no. They don't think it's polite.' I blew up at her. I told her, 'I'll call whoever I want.'"

A half hour later Natasha calls.

"Oh, you're back from Israel," she begins in a voice of innocent surprise. She asks me why Brian is so upset. "What can we do to calm him down? I am not to blame for what is happening. If you don't believe what I tell you, I can refund you your money."

She might almost be glad to do this, I think to myself.

"We want very much to believe you," I say. "Our only interest is to get this baby out."

She warns me to watch whom we speak with. "Be careful with Posner," she says. "He's a journalist. He may be looking for a story. I'm not worried for myself but for the babies. You know the Russians and the Georgians do not have a good relationship."

She says now that we have to be prepared for the baby to stay in the orphanage until the moratorium is lifted. "If we take him out now, we'll be put in jail."

"But how long could the moratorium go on?" I ask.

"A month, maybe more. It is impossible to predict. Even after it's lifted, it will take some time to process everything."

The thought of Kali in the orphanage is agonizing. If only the picture had come sooner. If only we had said 'yes' on the spot and cancelled our trip to Georgia, if only . . . would it have made a difference? But then we wouldn't have seen Kali, then we wouldn't have known how much we love him, then we wouldn't have known how urgent it is to get him out.

*　　*　　*

Brian comes home depressed. He says he didn't do well tonight in his show. "I can't stir up much interest for it thinking about the baby."

"I know," I say. "I've been feeling sick about it all day myself."

We pour ourselves a glass of wine and try to brainstorm what further actions we can take.

*   *   *

February 1, 1997

Although we feel a personal letter from Ted Kennedy will have the greatest influence, we know we need to contact as many people as we can. We've sent a second wave of letters and faxes out to a variety of senators and congressmen, both Republicans and Democrats, *anyone* that might have some clout.

*   *   *

February 4, 1997

A response today from Jesse Helms:

> Dear Mr. Hickey,
>
> Thank you for your recent letter concerning Kalipkul. Upon receipt of your correspondence, I contacted the proper authorities of the American embassy in Tbilisi. In doing so I have requested their careful attention and consideration of the situation, along with any additional information I may be furnished with, on your behalf. Just as soon as I hear from them, I will be in touch with you.
>
> With kindest regards, I am,
>
> Sincerely,
Jesse Helms

We also received word from Senator D'Amato's office saying that a letter was sent to the American embassy in Georgia, on our behalf.

We were hoping a letter from President Carter, along with one from Kennedy would move President Shevardnadze to help us. We were sure this is the kind of thing President Carter would be happy to support. But here is the response we received.

Dear Mr. Hickey,

Thank you for your recent letter regarding your efforts to adopt a Soviet baby. Although we appreciate all that you and your wife have done, President Carter has found that interceding in a case such as this is not successful. Every country has its own adoption laws, which are quite inflexible, and President Carter has no authority over these matters.

With best wishes,

Mary Ann Blanchette
Director of Correspondence

*   *   *

February 5, 1997

We're up in Garrison for the weekend. I drive to our closest deli, three miles away, to buy some milk. As I'm reaching into my pocket for the $1.19, the Indian woman behind the counter asks, "How is your baby?"

"My baby?" I say, looking up at her, surprised. I have never spoken with this woman about our plans to adopt.

"Didn't you have a baby?" she asks, smiling.

"No," I say.

"But I've seen you with a baby," she says.

"That must have been someone else," I say, feeling a shiver down my spine.

"No," she insists. "I've seen you carrying a baby."

"Well . . . I might be adopting a baby," I confide, "but he's not here yet."

"Maybe I dream this," she says and laughs.

I leave the store cradling my carton of milk in its brown, paper bag.

*   *   *

February 7, 1997

From my window, I see a light snowfall dusting the city streets. I'm having trouble getting myself in gear this morning. Feeling bleak. I'm really worried that things could take even longer than we thought. Senator Warner's office contacted us. They said that they received word from the American embassy in Tbilisi that the adoption policy in Georgia was being revised, but as soon as foreign adoption is approved again, they will make every effort to handle our case as swiftly as possible.

As soon as when? I wonder. What if it isn't approved for months?

We also received a letter from Natasha offering to change us to a different program. It's obvious she doesn't believe the moratorium is going to be over soon.

Doesn't she understand that *we love Kali? We're not going to abandon him.*

*   *   *

February 8, 1997

Ted Kennedy's office has refused to help. They referred us to Senator Moynihan in New York. We've already contacted Senator Moynihan. His office sent us a form letter, repeating the same pat response we received from the State Department. Brian called both Kennedy's office and Carter's office back again and pleaded with them to reconsider, but no luck. This is a huge disappointment. We were really banking on both of them. How are we going to find someone with their kind of prestige and influence to get to President Shevardnadze?

Brian says he's learned that it is Mrs. Shevardnadze who has instigated the moratorium. It seems she made a speech imploring Georgians not to allow "rich foreigners" to take advantage of the country's difficult times by taking away her children. Ironically, we are appealing to her husband to grant us the exception.

I can understand she doesn't want to lose her country's children, but if there are children that the country cannot take care of—Dodo says that very few Georgians are adopting—isn't it better to give them to people who can provide a home, rather than punish the children? I wonder if I should write a letter to Mrs. Shevardnadze? Of course, what seems logical and humane to me may not look the same way to her. It's a delicate matter how to make one's point and yet not appear to criticize the country, or pretend to know its situation.

Natasha promises that Kali is still getting the "special" formula. But a baby needs so much more than formula.

Hope

February 9, 1997

Our new hope now is with Congressman Gilman from Rockland County. This is the same congressman Brian didn't even think was important enough to contact. It turns out that Gilman is the chairman of the International Relations Committee, and it turns out we have a *personal* contact into his office. A few months ago, Brian hired an older man, Joe O'Connor, to help him at his day job. All the other candidates for the job were young, and everyone else in the office is fairly young. Brian didn't know why, but he just got a positive feeling from this man. Apparently, Joe served on an economic advisory committee with Gilman and knows him and his staff. Joe says Gilman is a good man and will help if he can. We've heard through his office that the chairman of the Georgian parliament is coming to Washington in a couple of weeks. We're hoping that Gilman will speak to him on our behalf.

*   *   *

It's close to midnight when we get a call from Tbilisi. It's from the vice-consul of the American embassy, Richard Thompson. I'm shivering in my nightgown, more from nervousness than cold, as I press in close to Brian, who has picked up the phone in the living room.

"Unfortunately, we cannot intercede in the affairs of a foreign government, and we cannot act to favor one American citizen over another," he says in a bureaucratic-sounding Southern drawl. "We expect that there will be parliamentary hearings in mid-February on the issue of foreign adoption. We are hoping they will recommend a change in the law. But I visited the orphanage today . . ."

He's seen the baby in the orphanage! I grab the receiver from Brian. "How is he?" I ask, holding my breath.

"He looks healthy and alert," Thompson says with more feeling. "It may not compare to American standards, but it's the best orphanage in Georgia. The nurses seem attentive."

It's a tremendous comfort to hear this, though in the same moment I can't help thinking the nurses have to be attentive with the vice-consul of the American embassy visiting.

Still, we are so grateful that Mr. Thompson went to see Kali. Brian thinks that Gilman's office must have called.

*   *   *

February 12, 1997

Kali is four months old today. It's been a month since we've seen him. Does he understand on some level that we are doing everything we can to get him out?

I keep writing his name and playing with numbers. I'm thinking of changing the spelling of Kali to Cali so that his name reads—*Christopher Cali Odon Hickey*. In numerology, the numbers add up to a 3, the number of the artist. Also, Kali with a *K* brings up associations with the Indian goddess of love and death. He doesn't need that.

*   *   *

Natasha calls. Her tone is soft and conciliatory. She says the letter she sent us about switching adoption programs was a form letter she sent to all prospective Georgian parents.

She says she knows we are not going to be dissuaded. Yesterday, she had Brian write a letter (which *she* faxed) to the minister of education in Georgia, appealing for his intervention in our case.

"I almost cried when I read Brian's letter," she says to me now. "Hopefully, it will help . . . but in any case, I think the ban will be lifted within four weeks."

Four weeks is an eternity, I think. Even though the American embassy and Natasha are trying to convince us that the orphanage is not so bad, how good can it be? How good can any orphanage be just by definition?

"Is there any chance we can we get him out of the orphanage before that?" I ask.

"I don't know. He's still getting his 'special' formula."

"But do you think they hold the babies in the orphanage and talk to them?"

"Oh yes," she says a little too automatically. "And then Dodo goes to visit."

"Does the baby still have his dalmatian?"

"What?" she asks.

"We left a little stuffed dog with him at the hospital. It will give him something soft to have next to him."

"I will ask Dodo," she says.

* * *

Gilman's office says they are hand delivering two copies of Brian's letter, along with the whole package of photos we put together, to the *minister of education*, who, in turn will hand deliver them to President and Mrs. Shevardnadze.

I keep seeing the baby's face. He's in me now. I can't imagine having any other child. *He's the one.*

* * *

February 22, 1997

The minister of education must have received our letters by now. Natasha says that he's been preoccupied by a school crisis in Tbilisi.

It seems so inhuman to hold on to a baby who's been given up, when there are people who want to care for him, and all because of some political, bureaucratic agenda. Mrs. Shevardnadze's good intentions seem abstracted from reality. Her own children, I hear, went to school in Western Europe.

Brian doesn't think it would be helpful to write her a letter. President Shevardnadze, if he gives us permission, may be doing it without her knowledge.

* * *

I've started reading a fascinating, but disturbing, research book about maternal deprivation called *Becoming Attached: Unfolding the Mystery of the Infant-Mother Bond and the Impact on Later Life.* The author is a psychologist named Robert Karen. It's out of print and the New York Public Library had only one copy, but luckily, I was able get it.

I've finished the first chapter, "Mother Love." Karen gives specific examples of infants who were abandoned by their mothers and the effect it had upon them. He also cites a documentary film made in 1947 by Rene Spitz, entitled, *Grief: A Peril in Infancy.* The film documents the physical, emotional, and mental deterioration that *rapidly* occurs when babies are deprived of a mother. The cure, according to Spitz in a direct appeal at the film's end: "Give mother back to baby."

I have to go teach. I'm grateful to have my students to focus on. Class always lifts me out of my slump.

*   *   *

February 23, 1997

We've just received a fax from the American embassy in Georgia.

"The moratorium was put in place through a presidential decree, and it appears that no Georgian official has been empowered to grant exceptions to the moratorium."

Letters are trickling in from nearly all the other senators and congressmen we've contacted, repeating the same thing, pretty much word for word. Basically, they're all saying there is nothing more they can do.

*   *   *

I read from Karen's book, quoting a Hungarian psychoanalyst, Michael Balint—"The wish to be loved, totally and unconditionally, is a primary need of human beings from the time they are born. If they don't get it, they spend the rest of their lives searching for it."

I have a picture of Cali on my desk. He's looking up at me so wide-eyed and trusting. Beyond the picture, on the windowsill, are six yellow tulips. The flowers are slightly open, yearning to open fully, but fragile and somewhat withered from the unfortunate overexposure of heat from the radiator.

Will Cali be able to recover from the original rupture and all the transfers he's had to endure—transfers from one place to the next, transfers from one set of faces to another? Once cut, a flower cannot reattach itself and recover its natural expression. But a baby can attach to another mother figure—as long as it's done in time. According to Karen's book, the "timing" seems to be the crucial factor. Up to six months, almost everything is reversible. After that, it's still possible, but much more difficult it seems.

I feel this tremendous ache in my heart for Cali, and for all children who have to suffer—through no fault of their own.

*   *   *

February 26, 1997

I'm sitting at the counter in a coffee shop on Ninth Avenue, trying to read a play that a friend has asked me to look at. I'm having trouble getting beyond the first few pages. Is it the play, or just that I can't concentrate? My eyes keep drifting to a little girl, sitting a few stools away, with a young woman. There is something about the little girl's quietness and large questioning eyes. I can't really tell if the woman is the girl's mother or a nanny. She isn't paying much attention to the little girl. She's absorbed in her magazine, while the little girl is sipping her drink with a straw. Is she having a strawberry milkshake? I wonder. I can almost taste it. Just the thought of that strawberry milkshake takes me back.

Shortly before my fifth birthday, I was sent alone to France to spend the summer with my grandparents, my father's mother and father. I was accompanied on the plane by Rosemary, a woman my mother had met in a travel agency. She was tall with short dark hair, and she spoke with an accent. I don't remember saying goodbye to my parents, or how I even got to the airport. I do remember crying and throwing up on the plane and Rosemary telling me not to worry, that she would wash my dress and help me put on another. Only I didn't have another dress with me. I don't know what we did, but I remember feeling very cold. For some reason, we had to make a forced landing in London. Then I remember being in the airport, and sitting at a table with Rosemary. She gave me a strawberry milkshake. I remember that it tasted sweet and comforting, and I felt better. But then Rosemary had to catch a connecting flight to Germany, and I was left with a stewardess.

The next thing I remember was arriving in Paris holding a little metal lunch box and wearing a sign with my name around my neck. No one was at the Paris airport to meet me, and I waited for hours. Finally, my grandfather, whom I'd never met, came to claim me. He had been waiting at the other airport, on the opposite side of Paris. He was a total stranger to me, with big black-rimmed glasses.

He didn't understand a word of English, and I didn't speak French. I was told, years later, that I didn't speak or eat for the first three weeks of my stay.

I remember vividly the little white stucco house on the outskirts of Toulouse where I stayed the entire summer with my grandparents. All the houses on the street were gleaming white, with little gates in front and lots of brightly colored flowers. Behind my grandparents' house was a small vegetable garden to one side and a flower garden on the other, separated by a narrow path. At the end of the yard was a small running brook. I remember a homemade swing, suspended by rope from a branch. I remember a tree that showered down green juicy plums. I remember a big white cat that sat with me on the back steps. I remember going to church every Sunday with my grandmother, sometimes in the local church and sometimes in the beautiful Cathedral of Saint Sernain in Toulouse.

I remember many things from that first summer in France, but mostly what I remember is my grandmother herself. She had warm dark eyes, a kind face, and a soft welcoming body. I can still smell her skin, sweet, like the flower garden she tended with so much love.

I soon learned French and forgot all my English, and when it came time to return to Chicago four months later, I didn't want to go. I loved my grandmother and I wanted to stay with her forever. I would only see her briefly, one more time. It was the following year in a hospital in Toulouse, just before she died.

*   *   *

February 27, 1997

Feeling upheaval. I know it has a lot to do with what I'm reading, and feeling powerless to come to Cali's aid. In trying to understand the consequences of deprivation, my own issues are coming up.

I call the psychic, Belinda.

"I'm afraid the moratorium may not end," I say, trying to keep my emotion at bay.

"I still feel Christopher Cali is meant to be with you," she says, her voice calm and reassuring. "I'm not good with time, but I feel it will be soon. You need to understand that you are connected to Cali on a soul level. If you are meant to be with him, nothing can stop that."

I burst into tears when she says this. I've had this secret, but deeply powerful, sense that Cali is the same *soul* that was trying to come through with the other two pregnancies, the miscarriages. I don't want to fail him again.

"Keep seeing yourself holding him," Belinda says. "Imagine a double of yourself who is in the orphanage staying with him. Then time won't matter. You are with him."

I feel so grateful to have Belinda as a voice of assurance. Somehow, what she says always feels true, even if I have no way of proving it.

*   *   *

February 28, 1997

I decide to phone Dr. Uberi, the wonderful pediatrician we met in Georgia. I speak to him through his daughter, Maka, who translates.

"Would there be any chance of your father going to see the baby in the orphanage?" I ask. "We're not getting enough information on his condition."

"One moment please," Maka says. I can hear her hand come over the receiver. There's faint mumbling in the background. She gets back on, her tone light and cheerful. "My father says of course he will go. You must call back on Sunday."

*   *   *

March 1, 1997

I call Georgia.

"My father saw Kalipkul," Maka tells me. "Baby is fine. A little sad, but that will change when he goes home with you."

"But he's *sure* everything is okay?" I press.

"Yes," Maka says. "My father says not to worry."

"Please tell your father," I say, "how grateful we are for his help. We're praying that we will be in Georgia very soon."

*   *   *

Natasha phones in the evening. "I spoke with Dodo," she says. "There was a meeting in parliament to discuss foreign adoption. Nothing definite was decided on the moratorium, but the good news is that your baby will be transferred back to the hospital."

Thank God!

I find myself dancing around the apartment and singing out "thank you" to everyone who has helped us.

Most of all, I thank Brian. He's been relentless in his campaign—calls and faxes to Zurab Zhvania (the chairman of the Georgian parliament and Shevardnadze's right-hand man), to Gilman's office, to the Georgian embassy in Washington, and to whomever he can think of. By now, everyone in the Georgian embassy in Washington, as well as the Georgian cabinet and all the key members of the parliament in Tbilisi, know about Cali.

*   *   *

March 5, 1997

The baby is still in the orphanage! The director of the orphanage would not allow Dodo to take him. The bastard! He says he has to have a letter from the minister of education.

We fax an urgent letter to Gilman's office. They, in turn, fax the Georgian embassy.

Why does this have to be so difficult? They know the baby is going to us. Why do they have to make this innocent creature suffer? For what purpose?

We call Natasha. Now she's saying that if our baby is allowed to go before the moratorium is over, it could create a "world scandal."

*   *   *

March 6, 1997

"What does she mean, world scandal?" Joe O'Connor, the kind man who's been our contact to Gilman, asks over the phone. "That's the most ridiculous thing I've heard so far."

"I know it's crazy," I say. "She says that if our baby is allowed to go as an exception, it would look very political. It's hard to know whose side she's on sometimes."

"Unfortunately," Joe says, "you're dealing with something that doesn't make any logical human sense, and as much as Gilman would like to help, it's important not to do anything that could upset the cart. I think of these kind of political, diplomatic relations as big chess games."

*   *   *

I find Robert Karen, PhD, the author of *Becoming Attached*, listed in the Manhattan phone book. I call to make an appointment. He has an opening for the day after tomorrow.

*   *   *

March 8, 1997

Dr. Karen is a reserved, slim, delicate-featured man who looks to be in his late forties. He leads me into a small, subdued room and invites me to sit on the couch. I ask if I can sit in the chair that is opposite him. I want to sit closer. I also want to be more in control of myself. I'm feeling somewhat shaky.

"How old is the baby?" Dr. Karen asks.

"Almost five months," I say.

"And where was he before he went to the orphanage?"

"It's a little unclear. I think he stayed in the hospital where he was born for the first month, and then there may have been some other place, and then he was sent to the hospital where we saw him. And there, even though it's not an ideal situation, there are nurses that seem to care about the babies. In the orphanage, I'm afraid, the conditions are much worse. Your book seems to suggest that up to six months, if the baby is neurologically sound, the effects of institutionalism and mother deprivation are reversible, but after that it gets more difficult."

"Yes," he says, "although . . . as I was trying to warn you over the phone, this is not really my area of expertise. That if you wanted to talk strictly about early child development, when is it getting late, how much can be expected when a baby hasn't had an established caretaker for *x* amount of time, I probably would suggest you speak to someone else. Yes, six months is a time people talk about, but it's not black-and-white. It's not going to be the same for every baby."

"I know," I say, looking away.

"You seem to be getting upset," he says.

"I guess your book has stirred up a lot of questions and concerns, and . . ." I let out an unwanted laugh, "maybe has brought up some of my own issues of mother deprivation."

There's a pause.

"May I ask you why you are adopting as opposed to having your own?" he asks.

"I had two miscarriages," I say. "I mean . . . there was nothing that said I could not have a child. The doctor said, 'try again,' but I guess it got to the point where if it wasn't going to happen naturally, I wasn't going to push things . . . and then, I don't know, I started getting pulled toward the idea of adoption. Strange things started happening. People I would meet, and then one thing led to another . . . and my husband and I got to Georgia. I almost feel it's destiny at this point. I feel as though there's some overall plan to all of this . . . though I'm not quite sure what it is yet."

Dr. Karen doesn't say anything, just looks at me intently. I wonder if he thinks I'm crazy to be speaking about destiny. Maybe this was a mistake to have come. "Is there something else you want to ask me?" I say, needing to break the silence.

"I'm still interested in hearing you talk," he says. "When you said mother deprivation before, what did you mean?"

"Oh . . . not that I was adopted, or abandoned, or anything like that," I say quickly, "but . . . I suppose I can relate to not having a mother be around so much. My father was around more than my mother, and . . ."

"You seem to be catching your breath when you say that," Karen says, "as though you had a heavy weight. Is your mother alive?"

I nod.

"And your father?"

"He died thirteen years ago."

"You say your mother was not around so much. Did she work?"

"No . . . not really, but she was out of the house a lot. She had friends, she had classes, and later, when I got a little older, she went on trips. I mean it's not that I didn't see my mother; I saw her, and she made sure I had good food and was well taken care of, and she sent me to good schools, and good camps . . . I mean, I wasn't neglected in that sense, but I guess . . . I guess from very early on . . . I never felt sure . . . that my mother *really wanted me* . . . I'm sorry . . . I don't know why I'm getting so emotional about this. I came to talk about the baby."

"It sounds as though you connect very much to the baby," Karen says, compassionately.

" . . . Well, it's just that I know the effect when there isn't that emotional security from the mother. I worry now what it must be like for the baby in the orphanage—not having one steady person, and if there's anyone there at all to comfort him at night. I mean five months is a long time. A night must be an eternity for a baby."

"That seems to resonate for you. Do you have some specific memory connected with that?"

A wall immediately comes up in front of my face, and I can feel a tightening in my chest and throat. The tears are burning behind my eyelids, and I feel as though I'm falling through space.

"I remember . . . I remember being sent someplace . . . I don't know if it was a few days, or a few weeks, but I remember the agony of the nights hoping that my parents were going to come and take me home. I guess I was about five or six. It was before we left Chicago for New York. My parents went someplace and for some reason I was left. Maybe it was some kind of school because I remember I was in a bunk bed, although I don't remember any other children, but I remember . . . staring at the wall."

"Yes?" Karen says.

My throat feels like razor blades. "Staring at the wall . . . trying to fall asleep, but I couldn't sleep . . . so I would walk out onto the landing. I remember my feet feeling very cold . . . and I would look down the staircase and wait . . . but no one would come."

*   *   *

I call Brian from the phone booth on the corner, even though I am only a few blocks away from home.

"How did it go?" he asks.

"All right," I say softly.

"Natasha called," he tells me. "She says the baby is back in the hospital . . . but it's looking pretty bleak about getting him out before the end of the moratorium."

"We have to go to Georgia," I say.

"What?" Brian says.

"I think we have to take things into our own hands, or else we're never going to get him out of there."

"I feel the same way you do, but it's not going to help to go now, and it might make things worse. We really need to be here now to push. We have to get the okay from Shevardnadze, or we'll never get him out. Let's just see what happens this week. Zhvania, the chairman of the Georgian parliament, is supposed to be coming to Washington . . ."

My face wet with tears, I hang up the receiver. I see that it has started to rain. I lean back against the wall of the glass booth and wait.

* * *

March 12, 1997

I had to cancel my class today. I'm sick in bed. Whatever flu bug I've caught seems to have taken a turn for the worse. I can't speak, can hardly breathe, and have a racking cough. I need to get better fast. Congressman Gilman is scheduled to lead a town meeting in Tarrytown on Friday. Joe O'Connor is arranging for us to speak with Gilman after.

Cali is five months old today. I can't believe two months have already gone by. I woke up in the middle of the night hearing inside my head: "History is often repeating the mistakes made by our parents."

Here I am, having to leave Cali the way I was left . . . so many times. Will I be able to give Cali the emotional security that he will desperately need after such a beginning?

The day after seeing Robert Karen, I called Jay Belsky, an expert on institutionalized children that Karen recommended and whom he refers to in his book. Belsky said the sooner we can get the baby out, the better, but not to get too overanxious about delays. Once the baby is with us, he warned, don't try and overcompensate with more food, or more stimulation. "Children catch up in their own time," he said. He stressed the most important thing is to have a "stable, consistent, loving environment . . . and that the *mother be with the baby*."

I think to be a mother, to be a *good mother*, demands the ultimate of . . . I shouldn't say sacrifice because that implies martyrdom, but it seems to me it does require the ultimate expression of unselfishness. Do I have that unselfishness in me? Do I have enough of the *good mother by feminine inheritance*, by instinct?

Brian calls me from work. "Are you feeling any better? I have some news that might cheer you up. Gilman just finished meeting with the Georgians."

I quickly prop myself up on my elbow, my head throbbing. "And?" . . . I cough out.

Yes!

March 12, 1997

"They said yes!" Brian exclaims. "Gilman asked if an exception could be made for our baby, and they said yes."

I can feel my fever suddenly breaking into a cold sweat. "Who said yes?" I whisper.

"Both Chairman Zhvania, *and* President Shevardnadze," Brian says.

"Are you sure?"

"Yes. Zhvania is in New York today at the Lowes Hotel. I'm going to try to see him. I'll call you later. Try to get some rest."

Oh God! I feel as though I'm riding a roller coaster.

*   *   *

"I wasn't able to see Chairman Zhvania," Brian says later from a pay phone, "but I did speak on the phone with Zhvania's assistant, Vaja. He's very familiar with the case. He says he was involved with helping to get the baby out of the orphanage and take him back to the hospital."

"So it's definite?" I ask. "He's out of the orphanage?"

"Yes," Brian says. "Hey, you sound better, your voice is almost back."

"Yea, you gave me the best medicine possible. When did this . . . Vaja say we can get Cali?"

"No date yet. I'm going to try to get David Soumbadze, from the Georgian embassy in Washington, to fax the minister of education in Tbilisi. We still have to have his signature."

I let out a raspy groan. "Oh, no."

"Don't worry," Brian says. "I'm sure there's not going to be a problem if the president says 'yes.'"

*   *   *

March 14, 1997

Still feel a bit under the weather, but I'm going to this town meeting tonight, no matter what.

*   *   *

Later: Town Hall, Tarrytown

Brian and I take a seat close to the front in the large crowded room. Congressman Gilman is late. I don't mind. It gives me a chance to meet and thank Joe O'Connor, who has been like an angel from heaven. He makes me think of an ex-astronaut with his white hair, blue windbreaker, John Glenn face, and Sam Shepard legs. In voice and manner, he strikes me as someone very gentle and polite—but also extremely determined. He's definitely out to help us get this baby. How is it that this *stranger* is playing such a major role in our lives? Brian gives Joe a pat on the back and says, "If it weren't for Joe, this never would have happened."

I'm thinking that if Brian hadn't followed his instinct to hire Joe, things would be very different, too.

Congressman Gilman, a short, stocky man with a full head of white hair and black bushy eyebrows, rushes to the front of the room. He apologizes for being late and immediately introduces himself as the congressional leader of the district. He says the purpose of this annual meeting is so that constituents can be informed of the issues that are being dealt with in Congress, and also to have a forum to ask questions and voice concerns. "What you think is very important to us," he says.

I like him—straightforward and personable.

Joe had put our name on the list for people requesting to see Gilman after the meeting. It seems almost everyone present wants to speak with him. Gilman says he will stay as long as necessary. He takes a seat and a long line forms. We wait until the end, when we can have a moment apart from the crowd.

"He's a beautiful baby," he says, smiling at the photo of Cali that we've brought. Then looking up, says, "We spoke to Chairman Zhvania about making an exception, and he said he would take care of it." Gilman takes a moment and looks at me thoughtfully. "But I don't want to see you get your hopes up too high before we have this in writing. I wouldn't want you go over there and have to wait for months. I've seen that happen."

"I know Gilman will do everything he can," Joe says to us in the car as we're driving him home, "but don't let that stop you from sending out more faxes to anyone you can. Don't let anyone who says there's nothing they can do make you hesitate to ask the next person."

"Brian was thinking before of sending a fax to the Pope," I say.

"Do," Joe says, with all seriousness. "You should contact the Vatican. The Pope loves children. The thing is that when you ask these people in power, you're doing them a favor, because if they can do something good, it makes them feel better and also makes them look better."

"Do you have his fax number?" Brian asks.

* * *

March 17, 1997

The phone rings as I'm rushing out the door. I let it ring and grab my keys, but then hear Brian's voice on the machine. I can hear hesitancy in his tone. I run to my desk to pick up the receiver. "Brian?"

"I'm afraid the news isn't good. The baby is back in the orphanage."

"What?" I cry out. "How did that happen?"

"I don't really know for sure. Natasha said she couldn't reach Dodo, that there was something wrong with the phone lines. She said that it was this guy, Victor, her coordinator in the Ukraine, who told her the baby was in the orphanage."

"How does he know?" I ask.

"Who knows," Brian says. "Dodo is somehow connected with him."

"We have to call Dodo ourselves," I say. "If Natasha doesn't like it, too bad."

We phone Dodo, but she's not there. We send an urgent fax to Chairman Zhvania's office in Tbilisi.

* * *

115

March 18, 1997

"You're going to get your baby," Belinda says to me over the phone. "I almost thought you were going to tell me tonight that you were on your way. I know your fear of abandonment and that you don't want to call Cali your own until you're sure you have him in your arms, but it's okay for you to start saying 'my baby.' Corinne needs to say, 'this is my baby.'"

"I really am thinking of him as my baby," I say.

"There's so much love in your voice when you say that," Belinda says.

"In a way," I say, "It *has* been like a pregnancy. I'm ready now. I don't want to wait any longer."

*   *   *

March 19, 1997

We receive a fax from the chairman's office in Georgia. It reads: "Issue of orphanage resolved."

Vaja

We call the Georgian embassy in Washington.

"I believe you will be allowed to go to Georgia very soon," says David Soumbadze. "I will call the chairman's office in Tbilisi tonight and get back to you over the weekend."

*   *   *

March 23, 1997

No word from David Soumbadze.

We try to reach Dodo again. This time she answers. She's at home, sick with the flu. Everyone seems to be under the weather. I can hear an all too familiar racking cough.

"I don't know when they will give permission for baby to go," she says with effort, "but I think will be soon. Your baby may be only one permitted to go. It is possible that foreign adoption may be completely shut down." Then she says, "baby has flu."

"Flu?" I say, alarmed. "Is he very sick?"

"He will be all right," she says, barely able to get the words out. "Everyone in Georgia has flu."

*   *   *

March 28, 1997

We finally reach David Soumbadze. He apologizes for the delay in getting back to us, but says that the good news is that President Shevardnadze has given orders to the ministers of health and education to release the baby.

I can hardly contain myself. "Are you sure?" I ask.

"That is the word we have received," he says.

I call Natasha. "Cali is being allowed to go," I say in a tone that brooks no objection.

"Oh yes, I know that," she says casually.

I take a breath. "Okay," I say, "but I just want you to know that we don't want to be held up by any more unnecessary delays. The baby has the flu. If we're given word to go, we're going and that's it."

"I am not delaying anything," she throws back angrily, "but I cannot allow you to go under my supervision until I get written confirmation." Then she says, matter-of-factly, "The moratorium will be coming to an end soon in any case, and the other babies will also be released."

I hope it's true that the moratorium will be coming to an end soon, for the sake of the babies and for the parents who are waiting, but that's not the information we're getting from the Georgian embassy in Washington, or from Dodo. It doesn't matter. All that matters now is Cali.

*   *   *

March 29, 1997

We stay in Garrison for the weekend. We drive up to the mall in Poughkeepsie and spend much of the day shopping for the baby. We haven't bought anything up until now. We've been feeling too superstitious, but soon Cali will be here and we need to be ready.

We buy a car seat, a fold-up bed that can also be converted into a playpen, and a stroller. For the trip home from Georgia, we buy the baby pajamas, undershirts, socks, jacket, a baby bottle, pacifier, a changing bag, and a Bjorn

Bag harness to carry him in. Blankets and toys we have. We still need to get diapers, formula, and a first-aid kit.

We had hoped we might be there by Easter Sunday, which is tomorrow, but barring any further obstacles, next Sunday.

*   *   *

March 31, 1997

We receive a call from David Soumbadze.

"You can go to Georgia," he says. "Congratulations." This ecstatic news is in the morning, but then everything goes downhill after that.

I phone Boris to arrange for the airline tickets. "I can't do anything until I have an exact return date," he says.

I call Dodo. "We can go," I say excitedly. "We're coming. We just need to know how long it will take, so that we can book the return."

She sounds alarmed. "Papers will take two more weeks," she says.

"Don't worry," I say, "the Georgian embassy in Washington has given us the OK, and the American embassy in Tbilisi has already told us that it will only take two days on their end."

I can hear her alarm turning to annoyance. She says, almost passively, "I will go to chairman's office today to see what is next paper needed."

I don't understand her tone.

We need new photos for the visas. Natasha says that she has to have them right away. Only, we are still upstate in Garrison; it's beginning to snow very hard, and now our car won't start—the battery is dead!

While we wait for Triple A to arrive, Brian sets up the playpen/bed that we had driven an hour away to buy the day before and had taken much of the afternoon to select. As Brian is about to put together the last few pieces, he notices in the instructions that the playpen is safe for babies *only* up to three months of age.

By the time Triple A arrives three hours later, there's over a foot of snow on the ground. It's not going to be possible to get passport pictures now. I have to teach a class in Manhattan, which I'm already late for.

When I get home from the New School, there's no message from Natasha and no fax from Tbilisi confirming what the Georgian embassy here had said.

At midnight, we phone the American embassy in Tbilisi. We're told that Richard Thompson, whom we normally deal with, is on vacation. His assistant, Maria, does not know anything about our case being an exception to the moratorium. As far as she is concerned, there are *no* exceptions.

"Richard will be back on Thursday," she says. "I will ask him about it then."

Today is only Monday.

* * *

April 8, 1997

"I've had it," I cry out to Brian, turning from the living-room window, where I've been looking out at the steady rain. "Everyone is giving us double talk. I can't live each week in suspension. Vaja said on Friday that he would send a fax to say that we could come. It's now Tuesday. There's no fax. I wanted to get our baby as young as possible so that he wouldn't have to suffer the neglect and damage of an institution."

"What do you want to do, give up?" Brian harshly snaps back. He's kneeling beside the coffee table, a stack of mail and bills in front of him, trying to make some order.

I hate him for asking that. I hate his feigned calm. I hate *everything* right now. I want to scream, punch, kick. I go into the kitchen, open the refrigerator, and then slam it shut. I stampede back into the living room.

"The baby will be six months old this weekend," I say. "He's lying in an orphanage, and no one seems to care—from Mrs. Shevardnadze down to the chairman, and all the ministries."

Brian stands up. "Look," he says, "we're doing everything we can."

"It's not enough!" I cry.

He moves toward me and puts his arms around me. "I feel the same way you do, but it's not going to do any good to get stressed out."

"But why can't they understand that it's the life of a human being? Every day counts, every day he has to stay there could have consequences . . . for his whole life."

The dogs jump up and down, wanting to be part of the embrace. We pick them both up and hold them between us.

The phone rings. It's Natasha. "You should wait until next week," she says. "Vaja is saying the same thing. Tomorrow is a national holiday in Georgia, and this will delay things. If you leave this weekend, you will just have to wait there an extra week."

I feel like a blowtorch. They all tell us things, things we *want* to hear. We believe them—because we *need* to believe them. We want to trust, but then the things they say don't happen. I feel so betrayed.

*   *   *

April 9, 1997

I dream that I'm on the phone. I hear Cali's voice, his baby sounds. "This is your mother, Cali," I say softly to him. "This is your mother." I'm aware of feeling happy to hear Cali's voice, but I'm also sad, very sad.

Another fax arrives from Vaja.

Dear Mr. Hickey,

Dr. Vasaladze has started today adoption procedures from the Ministry of Health and she needs to get through Ministries of Education and Justice. I think she will need another ten days to finalize documents. I was informed that you are already planning to travel to Georgia. I think that better would be if Dr. Vasaladze and I will go on with the documents and then inform you when your arrival will be necessary. I am afraid that your presence will play rather negative than positive role now. It frightens our ministries and may create problems for us in dealing with them, because a lot of American citizens are looking forward to adopt child in Georgia. Dr. Vasaladze will inform me and you about her further steps on Thursday, and then I will be able to tell you more.

Oddly, in the very next paragraph, he writes:

If you think that your presence would help adoption procedures or would be better for you, you are welcome to arrive in Georgia. Next week, Parliament will start considering draft Law on Adoptions, which will also help us.

Yours,
Vaja

How can he say he was "informed that we are already planning to travel to Georgia," when he himself was the one who gave us the "go ahead" to come?

*   *   *

Later I share with a colleague at the New School the insanity that has been going on.

"I'm feeling *murderous*," I say, trying to sound tongue in cheek.

My friend laughs. "God is preparing you for motherhood. A mother would kill to protect her child."

*   *   *

April 12, 1997

Natasha calls and says that she has received the baby's medical report and that she will send it to us via Federal Express. "You need to sign it immediately and send it back to me." There's a pause. "I have to warn you that it does not sound good," she says.

A wave of fear floods through me. "What do you mean?"

"I told you in the beginning that they would not allow a healthy baby to leave Georgia," she says. "They have to write down many problems."

I can hear nervousness in her voice.

" . . . Can you find out what's true and what's exaggerated?" I ask quietly.

"I will ask Dodo," Natasha says, "but she has to be careful what she says on the phone."

*   *   *

April 13, 1997

MEDICAL AND DEVELOPMENTAL INFORMATION

Weight: 7,450 g   Head circumference: 42 cm
Length: 64 cm   Chest circumference: 43 cm

Diagnosis: perinatal posthypoxix encephalopathy: spastic tetraperisis, light form.

Psychomotor Development and Behavior of the Child:

The child is cautious. He shows adequate reactions. The child smiles in the direction of sound, leans forward to toys, takes toys in his hands, observes them. He does not pronounce sounds. There is a slight developmental delay in psycho-emotional sphere. The child watches objects, pupils of the eyes are normal. He shows reaction to light, conversion, accommodation is present. On the right side the eye opening is wider, the side of the mouth is lowered. His head configuration is braycephalous. Big cranial fontanel is open (1 x 1 cm), does not pulse. Holds his head easily, does not sit, does not turn over, stands on his tiptoes. He has a high muscle tonus of pyramidal type. Tendinous and periosteal reflexes are increased. Clonuses appear periodically. The child has to continue to receive medical treatment.

*   *   *

I call my doctor and get the number of a pediatrician whom she highly recommends. I read the pediatrician the baby's medical report over the phone. When I get to the part that reads "high muscle tonus of pyramidal type," the doctor asks, "Does he have cerebral palsy?"

"Cerebral palsy?" I say, thrown by her question. "No . . . I don't think so."

I get the number of another pediatrician. This doctor says the measurements are within the normal range, though the head circumference is borderline on the small size.

"Was he a preemie?" she asks.

"Yes, three weeks," I say. I tell her that the cord was wrapped around the neck at birth, and that oxygen had to be administered.

"That could not be serious, or it could be," the doctor says.

She asks if a CAT scan or a sonogram was done at birth, and if there had been any bleeding or any water on the brain.

"I don't know, but he did have an Apgar test and it was eight," I say, hopefully.

"There are two APGAR readings," she says. "One at birth and one five minutes later. It would be good if you could find out both."

She also mentions the possibility of cerebral palsy. "Or it may just mean he needs physical therapy," she says. "You need to find out how traumatic the birth was, and if it is possible to get an MRI now."

"I don't know if that would be possible," I say. "They've got sheep in the hallway of the hospital. Not that one necessarily cancels out the other, but . . ."

The doctor goes on, "if the baby were under my care, I would have him immediately in physical therapy, and I would monitor his head very carefully."

*   *   *

I call my friend, Viviane.

"You are really faced with the ultimate decision of your life," she says. "Would you and Brian be willing to go ahead if there is really something wrong with this baby?"

*   *   *

April 14, 1997

"I know they exaggerate," I say to Dodo over the phone, "but how much? I spoke with two doctors and they both said from the diagnosis that he might have cerebral palsy."

"No," Dodo says, with a sharp definiteness that I have not heard from her before. "I guarantee."

I remain sitting quietly at my desk. The question echoes through me—*Would I be willing if there was something really wrong with the baby?*

I glance over to the bookcase on my right. My eyes catch sight of an eight-by-ten photograph that is leaning against some books on one shelf. It's a picture of a thirteenth-century stone sculpture of Virgin and Child. The mother is seated and the child is standing with knees slightly bent and feet on the mother's left knee, supported by the mother's arm. Both mother and child are facing outward. Though they are not looking at each other, there is the feeling of great connection . . . of an eternal bond. The child's body covers the left side of the mother's torso—almost as if the child had been *born from the mother's heart.*

I look at my desk and at the picture of Cali in its blue wood frame. *Would I be willing . . .* ? It's not even a question anymore.

"*Yes*" I say, looking into Cali's eyes.

*   *   *

Action

April 21, 1997

Brian is leaving for Moscow today. By tomorrow, he'll be in Georgia with Cali. I feel an ache that I'm not going along with him, but hopefully, I'll be there by next week.

It occurs to me that it will be nine months from the time I saw Natasha in San Francisco, till the time we bring the baby home.

They've asked me at the New School to take on another class next year. That would mean being there four days a week. Do I really want to take on a heavier load with the baby coming? Cali is going to need all the love and focus I can give him.

*   *   *

April 22, 1997

There's a message from Natasha letting me know Brian has arrived safely in Tbilisi and the number where he can be reached. I wait until midnight (9:00 a.m. in Tbilisi) to call. A woman answers.

"He is sleeping," she says, in a thickly accented but understandable English. "I will wake him."

"Oh, that's all right, I'll call back," I say, but I can hear the receiver has already been put down.

"Hello, hello," Brian says a few moments later, in a groggy, slightly out-of-breath voice.

"Are you okay?" I ask.

"Yea, sure," he says, "but when you come, take business class from Moscow to Tbilisi. It was even more crowded than from Istanbul. There weren't enough seats. People were actually standing in the aisles the whole flight. It was suffocating. We'll definitely have to take business class with the baby."

"Have you heard anything more about the baby?" I ask.

"No, it was the driver who picked me up. I think Dodo is coming in a couple of hours to take me to the hospital."

I'm about to ask him where he's staying, when the line goes dead.

*   *   *

April 23, 1997

I anxiously wait until noon before calling Brian—to be sure he's in.

"I spent four hours with the baby," he tells me.

"Is he all right? How does he look?"

"He's gotten much bigger. He's very cute, but . . ."

There's a pause.

"Brian? Brian? Are you there?"

"Yea," he says, his voice muffled.

"What is it? . . . Brian?"

"We have to get him out of here," he says. "The nurses are nice, but they don't challenge him."

"Is he able to hold his head up?"

"He needs support."

"Does he smile at all?"

"He didn't at first, but then when I held him up in the air he started to."

"Does he seem sad?"

"A little, but then he also hasn't been feeling too well. His chest is pretty congested."

"Can you call Dr. Uberi? Maybe he can give the baby a thorough examination."

"I think we may have to wait till we get him out of here," Brian says.

"Why?"

"You know what happened last time."

"Nothing happened last time," I say, "and we were both glad we did it."

A pause.

"I think you should get here as soon as you can," Brian says, with quiet urgency.

*　　*　　*

I phone Natasha. "I want to leave for Georgia on Saturday," I say, firmly.

"Well, you can go," she says, "but nothing further has happened with the paperwork, and I think it would be better to wait."

"I don't want to wait," I tell her. As we continue to speak, she mentions in passing that she's had fathers go alone to pick up babies and that the mothers had difficulty later, because the babies were responding more to the father.

"Sometimes the mothers even have to go into therapy," she adds.

"That's it!" I say. "You've convinced me. I'm going!"

"Oh," she says catching herself, "but that was for older babies. Two years old. Not for a six-month infant."

*　　*　　*

April 24, 1997

"I'm coming," I tell Brian over the phone. "I've arranged it with the New School."

"Great," he says, "but just be prepared that it may not all happen in a week . . . I spent another five hours with the baby."

"He's going to be more attached to you than to me," I say, half joking.

"What are you talking about?"

"You're the mother now," I say, still trying to be light about it, but aware the tears are close to the surface.

"He knows the difference between a man and a woman," Brian says. "I can see how he acts with the nurses. He knows I'm not the mother, I'm there to play with him. He's waiting for you."

*　　*　　*

April 25, 1997

I tell my students that I have to leave for Georgia and that I won't be here next week. They all come up and hug me and wish me the best with the baby. I feel torn having to leave them this way, so abruptly, but what can I do?

I receive the same warm wishes from Lily and Pam in administration.

When I get home, I call Natasha for final instructions. "Will Dodo be picking me up at the airport?" I ask.

Natasha hesitates, "I'm not sure yet who it will be. Dodo had a family emergency. She had to leave the country."

"Leave the country?" I say.

"Yes."

"Will she be back? Will I get to see her?"

"I don't think so," Natasha says. "Olga will be taking care of you."

"Who is Olga?" I ask.

"Eke's mother."

"But how will I get information on the baby? Dodo was in charge of everything."

"You can ask the doctors at the hospital," Natasha says and then adds, "Brian has seen Dodo. He may have asked all your questions."

He has *not* asked all my questions, I want to say, but she continues.

"Brian is a little concerned because the baby is having difficulty holding up his head. We have to expect developmental delays, because even though the nurses have been taking care of him, he still hasn't been getting 100 percent individual attention."

Did she just say "100 percent?" That's the kind of absurd understatement that gets to me when everyone knows the reality is so far from that.

* * *

I call Brian. "Natasha says that Dodo has left the country."

"But she'll be back on Tuesday," Brian says.

"That's not what Natasha is saying," I tell him.

What is the truth? This has been the question all along.

* * *

April 26, 1997

Brian's brother, Michael, drives me to the airport. He and his wife, Susan, are going to stay at the apartment again to dog-sit. Michael has the hardest time finding the entrance to the Midtown Tunnel, and I, the great New Yorker, am no help. I nearly miss my flight. In my rush, I forget my coat.

It's a full plane. As I settle into my seat I open up the copy of *Newsweek* that the flight attendant just handed me. There happens to be a special edition on "child development"—from birth to three years old. The latest studies, according to this, confirm what I've been reading in Robert Karen's book, that environmental influences are as critical as genetic factors and that the most important development happens in the first three years of life.

> Only 15 years ago, neuroscientists assumed that by the time babies are born, the structure of their brains (had been) genetically determined. But by last year, researchers knew that was wrong. Instead, early childhood experiences exert a dramatic and precise impact, physically determining how the intricate neural circuits of the brain are wired."
>
> *Newsweek, Special Edition, April 25, 1997*

* * *

April 27, 1997

It's 8 a.m. in Moscow. I am stopped at Immigration and told to take a seat.

"Is something wrong?" I ask the passport inspector, a heavy middle-aged man with a flat face.

"Sit," he says, without looking up.

I take my passport and sit on the nearby bench. Eventually, a supervisor approaches—a younger man who looks a little more personable.

"Visa no good," he tells me.

"No good?" I say.

"No," the man says, "You have double visa. You should be here *yesterday* for first entry. You must go back to New York."

"Go back?" I say, quickly checking a smile. "I can't go back to New York. I've just traveled twenty hours. I'm on my way to Georgia to adopt a baby." Surely, saying this is going to fix things, *I think.*

"Then you must have transit visa," he says.

"A what? Please, I have a contact person waiting for me here, a Russian woman, who is supposed to take me to the other airport. If you will find her, she will explain. Her name is Nadya."

Finally, we locate Nadya, a petite woman who appears nervous and high-strung.

"Why Natasha didn't see?" she says, slightly hysterical. "They will send you back to New York."

Somehow, her getting so upset forces me to be calm. There is *no way* I'm going back to New York.

They don't send me back, but I do have to pay two fines: $75 to Immigration and $70 to the supervisor for "illegally trying to cross over Russian borders."

"Natasha must pay!" Nadya says indignantly.

My next plane is not until the evening. Nadya escorts me out of the airport and introduces me to Boris (another Boris), who will be my driver for the day and is to give me a tour of Moscow. He's an interesting, thoughtful man, and his English is exceptionally good.

Not only is today Sunday, but it is also Russian Easter, so there's very little traffic. It's a brilliantly sunny day, if a bit cool. Boris sees I have no jacket and lends me his. We visit the Kremlin, Red Square, and several Orthodox churches. Boris tells me that the situation in Russia is very bad. He says that many people are working without pay. Boris, it turns out, is actually a journalist. Because the economy is in such poor shape, he's afraid the Communists could win the next election.

*   *   *

Finally on board to Tbilisi. Surprisingly, I have a whole row to myself. Perhaps because of Easter it's not nearly as crowded as Brian's flight was.

In spite of some dramatic turbulence, I'm feeling calm and lighthearted. Easter—a day of rebirth—seems a positive day to be arriving in Georgia.

Georgia, Take 2

April 28, 1997

I awaken to a chorus of roosters. With one eye slightly open, I vaguely see red flowers swaying out the window. Brian is asleep beside me. I place my hand over his and drift off again.

When I wake Brian is gone and bright sunshine is slipping into the room. I quickly dress. It's a small room, with two narrow beds pushed together. Next to the window there's a bookcase crammed with yellowed paperbacks and textbooks of some sort. The room has a dusty, frayed appearance, but through the window I can see a little garden with three rows of bright red tulips. The door opens and Brian pokes his head in.

"Oh, good, you're ready," he says. "Our driver is here to take us to the hospital."

*　　*　　*

In spite of all that has happened since, it feels as though it was only yesterday that we walked down this long, gray hospital corridor. I feel my nerves starting to rattle as we approach the door that leads to the baby's room; my heart is pounding.

A nurse is holding Cali as we enter. I'm almost shocked by my reaction when I see him. Not that I didn't hope for this . . . but a part of me was afraid. I was preparing myself for the worse. The moment I see him, I feel this immense release, this incredible joy. It's almost as if the joy had been held in a tight box and was now suddenly being set free. God, he's gorgeous! I reach out for him. Is that a flicker of recognition I see in his face? Brian sees it, too.

"See, he remembers you."

Is that possible from an infant so young? I feel my heart is going to burst.

I take Cali into my arms. He's gotten much bigger. The puffiness around the eyes is gone, and the eyes are wide open, though the left eye does seem to turn inward at moments. Gone is the drooping mouth. I was worried about that. I can feel his head flat in the back, from all the lying down, almost like a pancake, but I'm sure this will round out in time. Brian says that in the few days he's been here, Cali has started to hold his head up. I can see he's not smiling much or reaching out for things, but he does seem attentive, and he does like me holding him. I sit on the bed with him. His eyes stay fixed on me. He coughs several times. I can hear a slight wheeze in his chest.

"Are they giving him something for his cold?" I ask, looking up at Brian, who is standing a few feet away.

"They've been giving him some sort of syrup and he's been getting breathing treatments," Brian answers.

"Well, that's good." I say, looking back into Cali's eyes. "We've got to get rid of this cold so you can fly on the plane."

The baby girl, Maly, who was in this same room with Cali in January, has been moved into the adjoining room. We can see her through the glass partition. She's standing up in her crib, holding on to the metal railing, staring at us. She has an anguished expression on her face.

"Why is she in there?" I ask.

"I think they were separated because of the flu," Brian says.

"What about the Greek family?"

"She's still supposed to be adopted by them, as far as I know," Brian says.

"She looks miserable. Do the nurses come in?"

"Yes, and they're very affectionate . . . with Cali, too, but they don't stay long and they don't stimulate them enough."

We stay with Cali for six hours. The only time he cries is when he finishes his bottle and wants more. Yet with his calmness, I can also see sadness. Thank God, we didn't wait another minute before coming.

* * *

The apartment we're staying in is on a quiet, narrow street in the Vake district. Our hosts, the Badridzes, seem very nice. Mrs. Badridze, who looks Mediterranean with her dark, expressive features, speaks English remarkably well. Her husband, a tall, lanky man, with white hair and a gentle, intelligent face, doesn't speak a word of English, but is eager to hear all that his wife has to translate. Our living situation here is modest, much more so than where we were staying the last time, yet the family appears to me highly educated. The daughter, who has her mother's striking eyes and her father's fairer complexion, is studying to be a doctor.

We have a peculiar arrangement here. The Badridzes lodge us, but another family brings and *serves* us our food.

"I think it's because the stove is broken," Brian whispers.

* * *

April 29, 1997

Back at the hospital, I'm holding Cali as the chief pediatrician, the one we met with in January, comes into the room. She is followed by Eke, our interpreter. This time, the doctor is immediately friendly. She knows we love the baby.

As she begins speaking to us, Eke translates.

"Doctor says baby was brought here to hospital when he was ten days old and he weighed only 2.2 kilos."

That's less than four and a half pounds. This is the first we've heard that Cali weighed so little.

Eke continues. "But she says even that he was premature, he has developed and grown very fast. She says he weighs now almost nine kilos (almost twenty pounds). She says only thing wrong with baby now is that his thymus gland is a little enlarged and that he has a tendency to catch colds."

The doctor is smiling at me as I rock Cali in my arms. She continues speaking.

"Doctor says the baby has changed very much since Brian came, and now you," Eke translates. "She says he was much quieter before, but now he's starting to smile and starting to make sound and putting out his hand for things."

It's true, even since yesterday he's become more expressive. It's amazing. A day with the baby is such a full experience, so many changes happen. I feel the connection with him increasing by the hour.

He's doing better on his stomach today. He's not used to it and the effort is a strain, but he really is trying to lift his head. It's so obvious that what he needs is stimulation and challenge, and most of all—love!

Brian is totally in love with him. "I've never been as sure about anything," he says, "as that he's supposed to be with us."

I feel this wrenching pain in my heart when the doctor says the baby may have been in the orphanage for two months.

"Two months!" Brian and I repeat, shocked. We were told it was three weeks.

*   *   *

Era, the full-bodied, quick-to-laugh woman who brings us our meals at the apartment, is the wife of Zauri, our distinguished-looking driver, the same driver we had last time. Zauri takes us to the hospital in the morning and then picks us up in the late afternoon. Today, he also drove us to the Russian embassy where we met Olga, the mother of Eke and the woman filling in for Dodo. We needed to get an extension on our visas.

I almost got arrested at the embassy for taking a photo. A rough-looking man in plainclothes came to me, pointed to my camera, and said some words in Georgian.

"No Georgian," I tried to explain with a smile.

"American?" he asked gruffly.

I nodded.

"Russian embassy," he said, pointing to the square building across the street. "No photo. Big problem." He abruptly thrust his hand at me.

"Passport," he demanded.

He was not dressed in any kind of uniform, but he seemed to mean business. Olga had just gone into the embassy with our passports.

"Passport," I said, pointing across the street.

Brian, who had been walking down the block, approached. "We're not supposed to take a picture of the embassy," I whispered to him.

"Why?" Brian mumbled back. "You're on the other side of the street."

The man gave Brian a dirty look.

"Passport," he repeated in a menacing tone. He definitely meant business.

I could feel Brian bristling. He pointed to himself and said, "American Congress."

The man looked at Brian in his tee shirt and blue jeans.

"American Congress?" he said, sneering. It was obvious he didn't believe Brian.

Brian gestured for the man to follow him. Fortunately, the car was close by. Zauri was leaning against the car door, on the driver side, smoking a cigarette. He instantly straightened as soon as he saw us coming. I could see he understood there was trouble.

While Zauri did whatever explaining he could, Brian went into the backseat and rifled through his bag. After pulling out just about everything in it, he found the paper he was looking for, the letter from Congressman Gilman to President Shevardnadze with the large, bold letterhead, "United States Congress."

Brian handed the man the letter. The man studied the piece of paper intently for several moments. Finally, he looked up at us, made a stiff, disapproving gesture, and said, "All right," but then added with a threat in his voice, "No photo."

Fortunately, we were able to get a two-week extension on our visa for another $270 each. It's now up to $990. Olga laid out the dollars for this last extension. Eke let us know later that Natasha was covering the cost. Brian and I didn't expect this. We're grateful.

We're still waiting for the signature from the minister of education, the same minister of education who, two months ago, hand delivered our dossiers to the Shevardnadzes and told Congressman Gilman he would do *everything he could* to help us.

*   *   *

April 30, 1997

I had a very restless night, with all kinds of weird dreams weaving in and out. My back is aching this morning. I wonder if the Badridze's would mind if we put the mattresses on the floor?

Brian goes to prepare tea in the kitchen. The Badridzes have a hot plate with one burner, a kind of large Bunsen burner, operated by kerosene—their only cooking system. The fumes are strong and it feels unsafe, but we're getting the hang of how to use it.

*   *   *

Later at the hospital, Cali is quiet. Every so often, he has a kind of faraway, forlorn look that makes me wish with all my heart that I knew what this little being has been through and could somehow erase all his suffering. But most of the time, he seems calm and content. The nurses are always saying "good baby" . . . "happy baby."

He is still more engrossed in his fingers than in toys. As he lies flat on his back, he holds them up in the air, and gently wiggles them. He watches them in awe and occasionally smiles, as if he is having his own private joke. I guess up till now his fingers have been his only toy and his main company. But he is beginning to respond more and more to outside stimulus. He's reaching out and reacting with little smiles. Whatever fears I may have had that it might be difficult for him to attach are gone. It's really hitting home that he is mine, and I am his.

The nurse brings us his stuffed-toy Dalmatian, which Dodo had brought home for safekeeping, fearing it would disappear at the orphanage. Cali isn't yet interested in it as a toy, but we pull the string and play the music, singing along as we wiggle the doggie in front of him— *"How much is that doggie in the window"*—and he seems to like this. We've named the dog Georgie.

With the doctor's permission, we take Cali out on the hospital grounds, for the first time. He seems slightly disoriented. His only experience with the outdoors has been when he was taken back and forth from the hospital to the orphanage. Not very happy associations, I'm afraid. It takes some time for his eyes to adjust to the bright sunlight. We sit with him on the grass. We have to support his body, as he can't sit up on his own yet.

Then a little miracle happens. His attention goes to a blade of grass that is moving ever so slightly in the breeze. He becomes totally fascinated and seems to forget his discomfort. He moves his focus back to his fingers, as if comparing them to the grass blade, and watches them in the most delicate and wondrous way.

He still has a cough, but I think sunshine and fresh air will do him good. It's actually warmer outside than in the damp concrete interior of the hospital. Sitting in the sunshine, I take off my heavy sweater. I lay back on the grass, and Cali nestles his face against my exposed skin. He falls fast asleep.

It's so natural being with him, as though it has always been. There's this sense of no beginning and no end.

*   *   *

May 1, 1997

Until now, Cali has been asleep when we've arrived. Today he is awake and smiling when he sees us, as if he's been waiting. I have a hard time keeping back the tears.

"His face has completely changed from the first day," Brian says. "I didn't want to tell you, but he looked pretty depressed when I first arrived."

"You did tell me," I say.

Cali even laughs several times during the course of our afternoon. He's suddenly making all kinds of sounds. The medical report had said, "He doesn't make sound." We can cross that one out.

We see Maly through the glass partition. She is all 'instant smiles' and outreaching arms the moment the nurses go into her room or when she spots us, but the smile contorts into panic and screaming tears the second she's left alone. It's normal for a baby to cry when left, but there's a feeling of intense desperation. I wish there were something we could do.

In the afternoon, we take Cali outside again. He's starting to get some color in his cheeks. He's still sensitive to the bright light and moving air, but easing him into the outdoors, walking with him in our arms, will strengthen him for the long trip home.

When will that be is the question? We don't understand what could be keeping the minister of education from signing his release. One signature is holding everything else up.

But in spite of the frustration, we have been blessed in being able to get Cali out of the orphanage. When I think of the babies who are still there . . . no one permitted to see them. Not even Dodo.

*   *   *

In the late afternoon, Brian and I go for a walk. Overall, from what we've been able to see and observe so far, the city seems in better spirits than when we were here in January. The shortages do not seem quite as severe. More people are out in the streets. It's warmer, that helps, and usually there's electricity at night. Occasionally we have to use the flashlight, but not often.

We enter a nearby park. The grass is a bright, lush green. The trees are beginning to bloom, and wildflowers are popping up everywhere. The air is sweet and warm. Mothers are out with their children.

By chance, we come upon a narrow path that leads up a hill. We follow it and find ourselves climbing up another hill, and then another. We continue up past a complex of deserted buildings and an inoperable tram until finally, at the top of the mountain, we have a spectacular view of Tbilisi.

There's a lake here. People are walking around the lake; a few children are swimming, there's a canoe or two out. It's an idyllic setting, a world apart from the war-torn decaying remnants within the city below. I start to jog, attracting curious glances from the locals I pass along the way. A complete oddity in Tbilisi—a woman jogging.

*　　*　　*

May 2, 1997

Could not sleep again. Worrying about the baby and this whole insane situation. Vaja keeps saying that he will speak with the minister of education, but when?

As the days progress and Cali is getting more attached to us, it's harder to leave him at night. This is why I was unable to sleep. I kept seeing him, his smiles, and then lying alone in that hospital room.

The nurses are usually affectionate when they look in on him, but it's very uneven—the amount of time they give. It really depends which nurse is on duty. There is one nurse who stays in the room just to keep Cali company, but most of the nurses come in essentially to feed and change him; or check on him quickly, and then leave.

I'm not complaining; it could be much worse, but . . .

On a lighter note, I do like it here and love the people we are staying with—the Badridzes. They've been so accepting and sensitive to our needs. When I told Mr. Badridze I was having trouble with my back, he immediately dismantled one of the beds so that I could put the mattress on the floor. It was an effort for him, hauling the heavy frame to the shed at the other end of the garden, but he and Mrs. Badridze said, "No problem." Mrs. Badridze is always asking me—"How can I help?"

Zauri and his wife, Era, have been wonderful, too. Era was bringing us huge vats of noodles and potatoes for breakfast. After the second day, I asked if it would be possible to have yogurt and fruit instead (we had seen fresh yogurt in the market and it didn't look too expensive). The next morning she brought the potatoes, but she also brought the most delicious yogurt I've ever had, along with oranges and bananas. She was also making us huge lunches to bring to the hospital and rich, sweet cakes with every meal. We brought the sandwiches and cakes to give to the nurses, thinking they might not be able to afford these things. They graciously accepted them, but the next day brought *us* cakes, wanting to return the courtesy. Georgians seem to be extremely generous people.

Before heading to the hospital, Mrs. Badridze and her daughter, Nia, want us to see Old Tbilisi. They drive us up lovely green hills, high above the Mtkvari River. We park the car and walk over cobblestone streets, passing some sixth century churches and mosques. It appears to be quite an affluent area, enclosed by well-kept colorful buildings with high frontal arches and ornate wooden balconies. There's also a strong Islamic influence. There are Mosaic stone domes built close to the ground, which Mrs. Badridze explains were once used as steam baths.

"Tbilisi is known for its warm underground springs," she says. "This is where our name, Tbilisi, comes from. In old Georgian, it means 'warm waters.'"

We enter a carpet store and see some gorgeous Georgian and Azerbaijani rugs. I would love to buy one, but the rugs are expensive and we have very little cash on us. We have to make it last.

"It's lucky they don't take credit cards," Brian says rolling his eyes. He knows my impulsive, sometimes extravagant tendencies.

We visit the famous Orthodox church we had seen in January—Sioni. I have the same reaction as I had last time—of entering a genuinely *holy* place. There's such a spiritual atmosphere. Flickering candlelight illuminates Byzantine icons that seem to speak secrets from the soul. A small group of men and women are chanting and singing off to the side, their voices creating an almost unearthly quality. I would love to stay here a while, but we have to go. I quickly say a silent prayer for Cali's release.

*   *   *

When we return to the hospital, there's a call from Olga. Mrs. Badridze translates for us, as Olga doesn't speak a word of English.

"She says she spoke to Vaja and he says minister of education will definitely sign your adoption papers tomorrow. Olga says she will pick them up tomorrow evening."

To celebrate the good news, Mr. Badridze reaches into the dark wood cabinet next to the dinner table and takes out his homemade vodka, which he pours into three china teacups. We drink a toast, Mrs. Badridze miming a cup. "To your success and to your family," she says warmly. Mr. Badridze smiles along, encouraging us to drink up. The brew tastes more like eau-de-vie and is a little hard to swallow, but it feels good.

*   *   *

May 3, 1997

Cali is quieter today. He sleeps most of the time that we're outside. Brian carries him on his chest in the Bjorn bag and we walk around the hospital grounds.

The emaciated dogs we saw in January are still here. There seem to be even more of them now, some just puppies. They watch us from a distance, hungry and curious, but so timid their tails seem permanently to droop behind their legs. We throw them pieces of bread, egg or meat, whatever we have left over from our lunch. Usually, we have to walk away before they will venture forward. Even starving, they are too frightened to come to us. But today one is a little more daring. I throw him a piece of sausage. He grabs it, looks up at us, and eagerly scampers away.

*   *   *

On our way back from the hospital, we stop at the American embassy. We want to speak with Richard Thompson, the vice-consul in charge of visas and adoptions, who visited Cali in the orphanage. We need his cooperation now to expedite the American release so we don't run into further troubles with our visas.

Richard Thompson—round faced, blond hair, Southern accent, probably in his mid-thirties—sees us immediately and takes us into his office. We get right to the point and tell him that the minister of education promised to give his signature for the release today.

"I hope that's true," he says, doubtfully. "As you know, the moratorium is still going on. Everyone thought it would be over the beginning of May, but now there's going to be another meeting."

I feel my heart sink.

"When?" Brian asks.

"We're not sure," Thompson says. "It's an unpopular subject in Georgia. I feel badly for all these families who get their senators and congressmen to contact us on their behalf, because there's *nothing* we can do."

He acknowledges that it's only because of Congressman Gilman's 'direct' contact with the Georgians that an exception was made in our case.

"We'll try our best since this is a special situation," he says, "but I'll need everything in order so that I don't have to act the bureaucrat. You should bring Dodo's assistant to see me so that she's clear on exactly what papers and information we will need."

When we're out the embassy door, Brian says to me that at this point Thompson probably knows *less* about what's going on with this than we do, since we've been in direct contact with the Georgian officials. "Thompson's told me many times that he can't interfere in internal Georgian affairs. He only knows what they tell him, so how could he know what Vaja, or the minister of education, has privately promised us?"

I hope Brian is right about this.

*　　*　　*

Natasha calls in the evening. "The minister of education has not signed the papers," she tells us. "Olga waited outside his office for eight hours. She says that Vaja's assistant will call him again tomorrow."

Mrs. Badridze, who insists we call her Tzira, brings out the homemade vodka again. "It will help you sleep," she says sympathetically, putting down two teacups.

The drink and the good conversation take our minds off our problems for a moment. We talk late into the night. Tzira and her daughter, Nia, translate for Mr. Badridze. They seem such a close-knit family.

"We know everyone on this street," Tzira says, telling us about the neighborhood. "We all help each other."

"People here look at you so *directly* in the eye," I say, "even people you pass on the street."

"And why not?" Tzira asks, laughing. "Where *should* they look?"

Nia laughs, too. They love to laugh.

"Well," I say, "just speaking about New York, people feel a little uncomfortable having someone look at them so directly in the eye. I'm not speaking about friends, of course, people you know . . . but strangers. You might look at them for a moment, but if they look back at you, the tendency is to look away."

Tzira and Nia seem to find this odd. "So, where do they look?" Tzira asks again.

"Well . . . in the subway, for instance, people read, they glance at the signs, or they look at the floor."

They find this very funny. After a while, the subject turns to politics and of the Georgians losing the war against the Abkhazians.

"President Shevardnadze decided to end it." Tzira tells us. "At least in streets it is safer now."

She tells us the Russians used the Abkhazians to get the area for themselves, and it was really a war of Russia against Georgia. "Neighboring countries are always trying to take from us," Tzira tells us. "We have many things. Beautiful seaside, oil . . . Georgia has always had war. From Persia and Turkey and Russia."

"We are an educated, cultural people, but we are behind in many things," she adds mournfully. "We lost seventy years with Communists."

That's more than her lifetime.

*   *   *

"I wonder how they sleep," I whisper to Brian in bed. There seems to be only one other bedroom, with one small bed. I don't think anyone sleeps on the couch in the living room. They don't mention it, and we don't ask. They never seem to eat or drink. And I've been wondering when they use the bathroom; I've never seen *anyone* go in there. There is some mystery here.

"They're either saints or Martians," Brian says.

*   *   *

May 4, 1997

"I think we have to reach Vaja more personally," I tell Brian at breakfast. "I don't think we should talk to him about the signature, but speak to him directly about Cali. Didn't you say his wife is expecting a baby?"

"Yeah . . . soon," Brian says.

"I'm sure he wouldn't want a child of his to have to wait day after day, month after month, in a hospital. If it were suddenly *their* child who was being held hostage, I'm sure they would be going crazy. These babies in the hospital and in the orphanage are not real to them. Otherwise, they could not do what they are doing. They could not be human and do this."

*   *   *

At the hospital, Cali is the best he's been so far. He's lively—physically and vocally. We bring him into the next room to visit with Maly. The little girl's blotchy face and swollen lids show that she's been crying, but now she lights up. She holds on to the bars of her crib and smiles wildly.

I lift her into my arms while Brian holds Cali. I can feel Maly saying, "Take me, take me!"

The four nurses on duty and the ten-year-old daughter of one of the nurses come in after a while. We have a little get-together. The ten-year-old sits on the floor and takes Maly on her lap (things are definitely looser here than they would be in a hospital in the States), while we sit with Cali and the nurses on the narrow iron bed that is next to the crib.

The nurses speak hardly any English. The one word they know is "America." The communication is mainly in gesture and grimace, but it's clear they want to know about our life there. In a Charlie Chaplin-like pantomime, we act out life in America—the fast pace, darting from one thing to another, eating on the run, always looking at the watch, no time to rest—or even breathe. They find it very funny and we all laugh together.

Maly screams hysterically when we have to leave.

*   *   *

When we get back home, Tzira tells us that Olga called, and that Vaja says the minister of education will *definitely* sign the papers on Monday.

"But you must not tell anyone," Tzira adds, emphatically, "because it is exception."

It appears the moratorium is not going to end any time soon. I only pray that they will at least give the babies to the parents who have already been promised. I'm thinking of Maly who is supposed to go to the Greek family. And some of the American families we heard from, who wait day after day, in constant torment.

*   *   *

May 5, 1997

Cali is sick today; he has diarrhea and a temperature. He looks the way he did that first time we saw him back in January, pale and wan. The nurse on duty, a young woman whom we have not seen before, but who speaks a little bit of English, writes some words on a slip of paper and has us go to the pharmacy a mile down the road to buy some medicine.

We have to change the baby's diapers four times in two hours. But the bottled water we bought at the pharmacy appears to be helping him flush things out. By late afternoon, he seems slightly better, but he still cries intensely whenever I put him down. The nurse tries to assure me that he will be fine.

Fortunately, the baby is in a peaceful sleep by the time Zauri comes to pick us up, but I hate to leave him. I worry about him crying out in the night, and no one coming to his aid.

"I wish we had a way of getting to the hospital ourselves," I whisper to Brian.

*   *   *

We stop at the post office on our way back. Brian phones his mother, Lee, in Chicago to let her know that we will not be coming home as soon as planned. Lee told us that she would come to New York for our arrival so that she could help out with the baby.

I send a fax to Jim Lipton at the New School, apologizing for not being able to return before school ends. I feel terrible about this, but I have no choice. I have to word my note delicately, very careful not to mention the "A" word. We are told the phone system in Georgia hasn't changed since the Soviet era; the calls are still routed through Moscow and routinely intercepted by the government, particularly the foreign calls. We've been warned that if word got out, it would be impossible to get the papers signed and Cali out of the country.

We make one more call—to Dr. Uberi. He's out, but we reach Maka, explain that Cali is sick, and ask if there is any way her father could see him.

*   *   *

We arrive home to a message from Olga. Tzira translates. "She says she waited at minister of education's office from nine in morning until seven at night. He does not sign papers. He says to her he needs to meet with his 'Commission.'"

"This is insane," Brian says. "What commission? There's no commission. He's lying."

Brian is ready to hire the Russian Mafia.

*   *   *

We have another restless night. Even Brian, who normally can sleep no matter what is going on, is tossing and turning. I think of Cali lying alone in his room, perhaps no one hearing his cries. I think of Maly, too. How long can they let these babies suffer?

*   *   *

When we returned Cali was depressed. At six months he was unable to hold up his head, he didn't smile and he seemed to have no interest in objects.

His fingers were his playmates, and his only toys. The back of his head was "flat as a pancake," and he would scream in terror when we turned him over on this stomach.

When we brought him outside, he was at first disoriented, and had a hard time adjusting to the light.

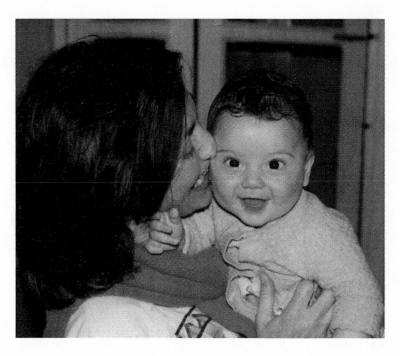

But each day he became more responsive.

Cali and dad "yucking it up."

Our poor starving friends wait patiently to share our lunch.

Cali naps outside behind the hospital.

Springtime in Tbilisi-Cali smells his first flower.

The Minister of Education

May 6, 1997

We've decided to go see the minister of education ourselves. Olga and Eke accompany us. Zauri drives us to the ministry office and waits outside.

We go up a dark and musty stairwell and enter a tiny windowless room on the second floor. Olga and Eke explain our situation to the secretary who is sitting at the desk. We don't understand what is being said, but the look on the secretary's face expresses concern and sympathy. She invites us to take a seat on the wooden bench facing her.

I soon have to use the bathroom. I'm directed to facilities at the end of a long, unlit hallway. The stench from the holes in the floor that serve as toilets makes me gag.

It's hard to know if the minister of education is in, or if we are still waiting for him to arrive. Several aging men in crumpled suits enter and exit the adjoining office. The men look our way in passing, but make no sign of acknowledgment.

Two hours later, we are taken into the adjoining room. Mr. Piradze, the minister of education, stands behind a large, dark desk. He is a big man, with a broad, stone face. We lean over the desk to shake hands with him. He coldly motions for us to take a seat.

He gives me a long look. I hold his gaze. Eke begins speaking to him and then translates for us. He looks back and forth between Brian and me, his face totally immobile. He does this for the first few minutes, but then after that, barely looks at us. Instead, he focuses on Eke and Olga, almost as if we are not there.

"Minister Piradze says he is not prepared for your visit," Eke says, translating. "He says many changes are happening with foreign adoption and they are still trying to decide on certain issues."

"Trying to decide?" I say, throwing a quick look at Brian.

"He says he will try to do what he can for you," Eke continues, "but he needs more time to consult with other ministers."

Eke goes on to explain that under the new law that is about to pass, orphans will have to be registered for six months before they can be eligible for foreign adoption.

"*Six months?*" I hear myself cry out, cutting a hole into the controlled tone of the room. By the expression on Piradze's face, I can see that he doesn't believe it is certain that we will *ever* be allowed to adopt our baby.

"Tell Mr. Piradze that both President Shevardnadze and Chairman Zhvania have already granted us an exception to the moratorium," Brian says firmly to Eke. "This was promised to Congressman Gilman."

Eke communicates the message.

"Mr. Piradze says that President and Chairman are not in position to make this decision," Eke says, turning back to us. "He says this is not their department."

"Please tell Mr. Piradze," Brian goes on, "that he himself said that he would do everything he could to facilitate this adoption, over two months ago. In fact, he was the first one to say that it *would* be taken care of. And every day since we've been here, we've been promised that he would sign."

Piradze denies having made any such promise. I can feel my whole body shaking.

"We were told by the Georgian embassy in Washington to come to Georgia," I say, trying to maintain some composure.

Olga seems to be taking all this in stride, her face a picture of resignation, but Eke's face has the strained, anxious look that I noticed the first time I saw her back in January. "Mr. Piradze says he will try to work in your favor," she says.

Try? I can't believe what is going on. I stare at him. His hard, blank expression has not budged. I feel like throwing the paperweight that is on his desk to crack that rock face of his. I wanted to be as civil and controlled as possible for this meeting, but now the tears are streaming down my cheeks, and I don't try to hold them back. Nor do I hold back my words.

"Tell Mr. Piradze," I say to Eke, "that it seems his word does not mean very much. It seems he must have been *lying* to Congressman Gilman. Tell him that my husband and I have left our jobs and our home, believing that we would be returning shortly. Tell him our visas are about to expire again. Each time it costs hundreds of dollars to renew, besides all the other costs that staying here entails. But tell him that the *real* issue is that our baby needs proper care and attention. He needs proper medical treatment. Most of all, *he needs parents.* To keep him in the hospital like this when there are parents waiting and wanting to give him a home is cruel and inhuman."

Piradze looks to his watch. I can see he wants to end the meeting. He says a few more words to Eke and then gets up from his seat.

"He says again he will try to do what he can," Eke says feebly.

"Ask him how long?" I say.

Piradze doesn't say anything more.

"How *long?*" I repeat.

I'm crying and shaking like a leaf when we walk out of his office. Brian puts his arm around me. Eke is by our side. She tells us that the minister of education told her that he liked us. A laugh escapes me at the absurdity of it all.

Olga moves toward the staircase. She motions to Eke and they speak.

"Let's go see Guram," Eke says.

We go up a flight of stairs to enter another tiny windowless room. A balding, fair-haired man is seated behind a small chipped desk.

"This is Guram," Eke says. "He works for minister of education."

The man smiles and extends his hand. This is another face entirely, warm and approachable. Olga and Eke begin to tell Guram what has just happened, but he quickly brings his index finger to his lips, gets up from his chair, and goes to close the door. He sits back in his seat, gestures for us to sit, and smiles again.

"Guram says," Eke translates, "that if minister of education does not sign, he will personally go get baby and give him to you."

*   *   *

"You know he couldn't do that," Natasha later says anxiously over the phone, when I repeat to her what Guram said. She's concerned that kidnapping could be on our minds. To relieve her fears and get on a lighter note, I tell her that Eke told us that the minister of education said he liked us.

"That's a good sign if he said that to Eke," Natasha says, her tone relaxing somewhat. "He doesn't say things like that easily."

*   *   *

When we arrive at the hospital and go to Cali's room, Dr. Uberi and Maka are already there. We had no idea they would come this quickly. The head doctor stands behind Dr. Uberi, her arms folded, watching carefully. Dr. Uberi insists these doctors are all his friends, but we still feel an awkward tension in the room.

He checks Cali's skull, his abdomen, and his reflexes. He opens the baby's diaper and looks at the diarrhea. He asks the head doctor about his medication.

Several times Dr. Uberi looks up to us and says, "Beautiful baby."

When he finishes, he speaks as Maka translates. He says that Cali is perfectly normal and seems in good shape. He says the rice drink he has been getting doesn't have enough calories—that he needs to get back on the Enfamil formula, and to start adding solid food.

His examination seems thorough, but quick. With the head doctor standing behind, it is difficult to ask too many questions, or to gauge how freely Dr. Uberi has spoken.

"Please come see us at our apartment," Maka says quickly as she is about to follow her father out of the room with the head doctor."

"I have a present for your father," I tell her.

"No, no," she says, "You just come see us."

Dr. Uberi has gone to see the baby three times now. Each time we've offered to pay, he's refused. And yet, the average salary for a doctor here is about $10 a month. How does he survive?

Tzira says that her husband is in charge of the research department where he works. He makes $15 a month. Zauri is the chief executive of a large factory, and yet he has to work as a chauffeur. As bad as the situation is now, Tzira tells us that it is a "dream" compared to the way things were a few years ago, during the war.

They have so little and yet give so much.

*　　*　　*

May 7, 2006

Now Brian is sick with a fever. What began with his stomach yesterday has become more generalized. I'm going to go to the hospital alone.

There's a call from Olga as I'm on my way out of the apartment.

"She is calling from outside minister of education's office," Tzira tells me. "She wants to let you know that Vaja is meeting with minister of education at this moment. She says she was asked to give baby's full name."

Oh, please, God, I say to myself.

Tzira continues. "Olga says, too, that Vaja's wife had her baby day before yesterday. He was born three weeks early."

I sit in silence in the backseat of the car as Zauri drives, wondering, is it possible that Vaja, seeing the vulnerability of his own baby, was moved to help another?

*   *   *

Cali still has a little diarrhea, but he looks better. He wolfs down his bottle of gray liquid and cries for more. I point to the bottle and make a sign to the nurse that the baby is still hungry. She shakes her head. No more food, she gestures, but she lets me know that I can take Cali outside.

I carry him in my arms. We sit on the grass. It's a beautiful, warm, sunny day. I take off Cali's sweater and shirt, leaving on only the undershirt, bottoms, and cap.

I take an orange out of my pocket. Cali is absolutely fascinated. He holds it with both hands and then laughs out loud at the wonder of it. His first ball. I open a jar of organic baby food we brought from the States. Sweet potato. I don't have a spoon, so I feed him with my finger. He loves it!

I see one of our dog friends at a distance, the tan one with the floppy ears and soulful eyes. We've come to know this one the best.

"I'm sorry," I call out. "I don't have anything today."

Cali looks at me inquisitively, wondering why my voice has suddenly gotten louder. The young dog cocks her head from side to side, stares at us for a few seconds, and then runs off.

I stretch out on the grass and place Cali on my stomach. I start to hum a tune that I learned as a little girl. It's a Russian song. I doubt I ever knew the words, but the melody has always stayed with me. There was a Russian violinist who used to visit my parents with his wife at our apartment in Chicago. I seem to remember that as he played for us, it was she who sang the song.

Cali lifts his head and stares at me. He loves when I sing to him. I sing another song from childhood, the French song that my grandmother used to sing to me. "Il était un petit navire. Il était un petit navire, qui n'avait ja, ja, jamais navigué, qui n'avait ja, ja, jamais navigué . . ." I rock Cali from side to side. He laughs.

How I love this little boy! I'm glad to have this time alone with him. There's a different quality to our connection today.

* * *

Back at the apartment, Brian weakly props himself up from the mattress on the floor. "How's Cali?" he asks.

"Hungry," I say.

"Hungry? Well, that's great. I wish I felt that way."

"Here, take some of this," I say, as I spoon-feed him some of Cali's medicine. "If it helped him, maybe it'll help you. He missed you."

"Really?" Brian says, his face brightening.

"Now you feel better," I say. "Instant cure. He's expecting you tomorrow."

I go for a walk in the park while Brian naps. This park has become a refuge for me. My two favorite moments in the day are when I first see Cali and then when I get to the top of the mountain by the lake. These are really hills for Georgia, but still, it's a good climb up. There's a mystical feeling up here, with the sun-drenched air and all the spring colors and scents. Every day there are more wildflowers in bloom. I've found a rock with a smooth surface, perfect for sitting and stretching out. I suppose I should keep my eyes out for "banditos" lurking in the bushes, but somehow I feel protected.

Banditos. Now why does that word come to mind? It's something my mother might say. I'm suddenly reminded of another place and time.

I'm twelve years old. I'm staying at a kind of bohemian, vegetarian health spa in the mountains outside of Guadalajara, Mexico. I've been here nearly a month, left off by two of my mother's "friends" who continued on with their travels. The young Mexican boy who works here has generously lent me his horse, and I ride every day for hours—galloping through the hills, undaunted by the possible dangers. I'm having the most exhilarating time—imagining all kinds of adventures and acts of heroism. I have totally left behind the screaming and the fighting of New York. I don't know if my parents have gotten the divorce they threatened. I do know my mother will be arriving any day, and then I will find out. The thought fills me with panic. I try not to think about it. I'm going to ride my horse, and then later, I will meet Nina, the young, blond-haired secretary of the resort. We will go skinny-dipping in the hot mineral baths. I will sing and do impersonations of the octogenarian guests at the spa, and Nina will laugh and compliment me on my abilities. And then she will confide in me her heartache over her fiancée; and then best of all, we will plan our trip she has promised we will take together to the Yucatan.

Some days later, my mother arrives. She's wearing a paisley short dress, large dark sunglasses, and a broad-rimmed sunbonnet. She catches sight of me. "Oh, come help me with my bags," she says. "You are my cowgirl." Cowgirl is one of her terms of endearment. That means I'm strong enough to carry her bags. "I can't carry a feather," she says, "or I'll be flat on my back for a week." She seems glad to see me—her manner so different than it was in New York. She hugs me. She tells me how well I look. "It was such a good thing I sent you here," she says. "You look the best you ever have. The air in New York is asphyxiating, and the heat is making people go crazy. Just look out for banditos here in the mountains." Surprisingly there is no mention of divorce. My mother lightly says, "We are going to meet your father in a few days."

I'm glad that Nina is in Guadalajara this evening. I can sit in the dining room with my mother and not panic about worlds colliding. "I used to worry about every leaf of lettuce you ate," my mother says, as she eats her raw cabbage and spinach salad. "You're so lucky to be eating this healthy food, free of poisons."

Later we walk around the bungalows under the brilliant starry night. My mother is definitely in a carefree mood. It's feeling good to be with her. My mother can be fun, a lot of fun . . . sometimes. Now she acts as though we are the closest mother and daughter. A little dog comes up to us. It's the Pekinese that belongs to the German owner of the resort. My mother pulls out a wrapping from the cloth bag she is carrying. Inside the wrapping I see the remains of a half-roasted chicken. "I forgot I had this," she says, giggling. The little Pekinese goes wild. I tell my mother that the dog is a vegetarian. She laughs. My mother loves dogs. She's always had a weak spot for them. "No one is going to make an apple out of an orange," she says, throwing pieces of chicken to the dog. The little dog goes for the morsels with the intensity of a tiger. "The poor thing," my mother says. "Vegetarian! He's starving. This is the happiest day of his life." I laugh with my mother in the shared moment of philanthropic conspiracy.

That night I saw my mother's warm, generous, rebel side, and I loved and admired it. We were close that night, my mother and I. I hoped it would last forever.

I've tried several times calling my mother from here in Tbilisi, but haven't been able to get through. I asked Brian's brother, Michael, who phoned yesterday from the States to call her for me and let her know what's been going on.

*   *   *

He Signs

May 8, 1997

When we return from the hospital, Tzira, Nicholas (Mr. Badridze), and Nia are waiting for us at the door, with big smiles on their faces, clapping their hands.

"Congratulations!" Tsira says joyously. "Minister has signed."

Brian and I throw our arms around each other.

"Vaja took minister of education to parliament to see Chairman Zhvania," Tzira tells us. "Olga says they locked the door and had a long meeting, over four hours, and at last Mr. Piradze signed!"

The homemade vodka is brought out again. This time everyone has a taste. We all sit at the dinner table.

"Maybe it was having his own baby that moved Vaja to go speak to the minister of education," I say.

Tzira shakes her head. "No, no, he promised. Vaja is a good man. If he promised something, you can believe. Only, he could not force minister of education. He had to wait."

The problem, as we're seeing it, is that everyone promised, but no one was willing to sign his name—no one, from President Shevardnadze down. We had their word, but not their signatures. With nothing in writing, nothing was official. Perhaps the minister of education felt his job would be endangered. We've been told that foreign adoption is extremely unpopular with the general public, and Mrs. Shevardnadze and the local press have stirred things up and made it much worse.

Natasha calls. Brian speaks with her. She says she's overjoyed to hear the news and that she will get our visas extended. She says she will have a better idea Sunday night how many more days it will take to finish the rest. I nudge

155

Brian to ask if there's any possibility to take Cali out of the hospital. Natasha says not until all the papers are completed.

* * *

Later in the evening we go visit the Uberis at their apartment. We had called them to tell them the news and they invited us over. Dr. Uberi and his daughter, Maka, greet us at the door and hug us over and over again. They seem as overjoyed as we are.

We meet now Mrs. Uberi and their other daughter, Eke. Mrs. Uberi is a neurologist, and Eke is a pediatrician, like her father—a family of physicians. Only Maka seems to have other aspirations. She says she wants to be a journalist. She has the character for it. She's lively and outspoken and full of curiosity.

We're led into the living room. As we were in January, we're struck by the art and beauty of the Uberi home. It's in such striking contrast to the decay and filth of the building.

We've brought the family a present. It's a large book on Impressionist painting that we bought for them in the States. They love it and are terribly appreciative. With great pride Dr. Uberi again shows us his uncle's impressionistic-styled paintings. They literally cover the walls. They are full of color and emotion and clearly suggest a gifted painter.

Maka tells us, "My father says, unfortunately, best ones were destroyed in the war three years ago."

Dr. Uberi shakes his head, but then smiles as if to say, "At least we still have these."

There's an upright piano, guitar, zither, and several other string instruments on one side of the living room.

"Who plays all the instruments?" I ask.

"My sister," Maka says, throwing her arm around Eke proudly. "My sister also speaks English."

Eke smiles shyly. Though she is the elder of the two and shares in her sister's sweetness, she seems quieter and more introspective, as does Mrs. Uberi. Dr. Uberi and Maka are clearly the extroverts of the family.

Dr. and Mrs. Uberi gesture for us to take a seat on the couch. On the table in front of us, a large spread has been laid out, consisting of various cheeses and breads, as well as chocolate, coffee, Coca-Cola, and French brandy. We are so moved by the family's generous hospitality. We wonder how they can afford all this. It is later revealed, as we speak about the economic plight in

Georgia, that Mrs. Uberi makes six dollars a month. Six dollars a month for a neurologist? I paid eight lari (five dollars) this morning for a package of Kotex.

We thought we might be receiving some medical advice about Cali, but instead, it is one toast after another. Dr. Uberi brings out a bottle of Georgian champagne, and we party till late into the night.

*   *   *

Tsira is lying on the couch with her coat wrapped around her when we return to the apartment at 3:00 a.m. We try to tiptoe as quietly as we can past her to get to our room, but the creaking floors give us away.

"Oh, thank God you are here," she says, sitting up with an expression of great relief. "I was so worried."

We had called her at midnight to let her know we would be late, but still she was worried. A mother.

"I will call Olga now and tell her you are back," she says.

*   *   *

May 9, 1997

I have been longing to hear Georgian music and see Georgian dancing, and I get my chance today. It is Victory Day in Georgia, commemorating the end of World War II. There's a big festival in the park, which, we learn from Nia who accompanies us, is called Victory Park. Septuagenarian and octogenarian war veterans, both men and women, are decked out in old uniforms, with medals and ribbons dangling from their lapels. Speeches are made; music is played. There is solo singing, and polyphonic singing (several men singing together as separate, distinct voices). There are groups of children dressed in vivid costumes performing traditional dances. Some of the children are extremely talented. In the stylized dancing, one can see the strong Eastern influence in the culture.

Brian and I are amazed to see so many posters of Stalin. Clearly, for many of these old-timers, Stalin, a Georgian, is still a hero. Even Mr. Badridze, who is the sweetest and gentlest of men, thinks that Stalin was a "great, great man," on par with Roosevelt and Churchill. We had a long discussion about it one night. Tzira and Nia do not share his view, nor, from what we can discern from this event, do most of the young people.

"Look," Nia says to us. She is pointing to a towering statue midway up a hill that overlooks the park. It is of a woman holding an olive branch in one hand and a sword in the other. It seems to me an image of the Great Mother, both nurturing and fiercely protective.

There is enormous reverence in this culture for the female principle. I think back to Eke telling us the story of St. Nino introducing Christianity to Georgia in the fourth century; and the stories Nia has told us of Queen Tamar, so beloved that she was canonized, so powerful that she is referred to as a *king*. Whenever Georgians speak of her, she seems totally present in their hearts, almost as if she were still alive. Yet they are talking about the twelfth century, three to four hundred years before Columbus came to America. Queen Tamar ruled over Georgia in this *golden age* when poetry and art flourished. The reverence for poetry remains.

On the other hand, it seems to be a very patriarchal society, with very conservative rules—in many ways, much closer to the East than to the West. For instance, Nia tells us that it's not really accepted for young men and women to live together before marriage. She says that girls were not allowed to wear pants to school until a couple of years ago. We've noticed that most women seem to dress up to go out, even to go to the market or to the park, and that the men and boys hang out together, without the women. One can see a whole group of men walking arm in arm down the street. Nia tells us that in certain parts of Georgia, in the mountains, the young men still kidnap girls to be their wives.

* * *

May 10, 1997

Today, after leaving the hospital, Dr. Uberi's daughter, Maka, and her cousin Nino meet us to go for a walk. Nino, a very pretty girl of about twenty, with strawberry blond hair looks remarkably like a young Meryl Streep. I tell her so and ask her if she's familiar with the American actress. "Oh yes," Nino says, blushing, "she is so wonderful." Nino is from Abkhazia, where she was studying law at the university, when the war there broke out. "We were on our way to seaside for holiday. It was big surprise. We did not expect."

Maka tells us that she was also in Abkhazia at the time. "My father went there with a gun to get me out."

"It was terrible," Nino adds, "bombs were falling, our neighbor was killed, we had to leave everything. It is very sad. Abkhazia is most beautiful part of Georgia, very European. Only ten percent of people there wanted to separate, but the Russians were behind them. We could not win against such a big country . . . but someday, I hope we will be together again."

We walk for hours, all the way to the Old City and back, mostly by way of Rustaveli Boulevard. Brian and I are used to long hikes, but we're surprised that the girls are willing to walk so long. Thinking they might be tired, but too polite to say so, we offer to pay for a taxi. Maka and Nino say, "No, you are our guests." If there is anything to be paid for, they want to do the paying. When I go into a store to get a bottle of water, Nino *insists* on buying it.

We pass the carpet store in the Old City. The storeowner says a film is being shot in the next room and invites us to watch. It is based on *One Thousand and One Arabian Nights*, and he boasts that it's starring a very famous Georgian actress, named Nino. (Nino and Eke seem to be extremely popular names here. Every family seems to have one!). The actress is stunningly beautiful with what I think of as a very specific Georgian look—light skin, black hair, thick black eyebrows, and large dark, ancient eyes.

It's a very simple set up—one actress, one light, and one camera. At one point, a carpet catches fire from the overheated light, but fortunately, the flame is quickly put out, and the filming continues.

*   *   *

May 11, 1997

Does Cali know today is Mother's Day? He gives me an extra special welcome when I enter his room. He keeps smiling at me, as if to say, "Oh, so this is your first."

He's almost able to roll over now. He's starting to feel at ease on his stomach. It would seem the most natural thing, but not for a baby who's been lying on his back for six months. He's also kicking his legs now and reaching out his arms toward me so I'll pick him up.

It's so funny to watch him laugh at his fingers. He has his own little stories going on in his head. He clearly has a sense of humor. "He's laughing," Brian says, in a Yiddish accent imitating Jackie Mason, "because he just told himself a better joke, than he told us."

"He picked the right father to clown with," I tease Brian.

I wonder if Michael was able to reach my mother. I haven't heard anything. She may not have really noticed our absence until today. I usually call her on

Mother's Day. Even though it seems like months to me, in reality I've only been gone two weeks. For my mother who is long-distance traveler and long-staying traveler, two weeks is not very long. When I was in high school, she would go off for months—long trips to exotic places: India, Nepal, Afghanistan. It might be three weeks before my father and I would get a postcard with a return address such as "Poste Restante, Kabul." My mother loved adventure.

Will the relationship with my mother be different when I come back with a baby? Will grandmotherly heartstrings be pulled? She always told me that she was closest with her own grandmother.

* * *

May 12, 1997

Cali is seven months old today!

We're praying that the paperwork will be finished in the next few days. It's been such a rich experience being here, but now I want to go home with my baby.

I had a dream last night—something about two children. This is the second night in a row that I've had this dream. There was something about a blood transfusion . . . and *rescuing* two children.

Am I one of the children?

There is a part of me, the child part of me that has always been able to adjust to any place, any situation—any home. This adaptability served me well and brought into my life many experiences and many wonderful people. Yet there's another part of the child that never quite felt at home, that never quite felt she belonged. There was always the slight ache—for something that was *missing*.

If only I can give Cali that sense of *belonging*, and the confidence that he is really *wanted* . . .

* * *

Cali is wailing when we arrive at the hospital. To our horror, there's a string wrapped around his neck! Someone tied his little rattle toy to the railing behind his head, but now the string is twisted around his neck. His pajamas and the sheets are soaking wet; he must not have been changed for hours.

We quickly undo the string, take off his drenched top and bottom, discard his soggy diaper, and over his screams clean and dress him as fast as we can. Then I rock him in my arms until he's soothed.

"I've seen this happen to Maly, too," Brian says, referring to the string.

Usually when we arrive in the morning, one of the nurses comes in to say hello and brings in a bottle, but this morning no one is here. I can't prepare him a bottle because I have no way of boiling the water.

I feed Cali some carrot puree that I've brought with me, and then we take him outside. We're surprised when we return and there still isn't a nurse or doctor on the entire floor. I go look for the blond-haired woman who normally sits in the front office near the entrance. At least she's there. I try to communicate through gesture that the baby hasn't had his bottle and that I can't find a nurse.

She's not able to find anyone, either. She keeps making a sign of surprise. Finally, she leads me to a cubbyhole, where we boil water in a chipped pan on a very corroded-looking hotplate.

Zauri arrives just as I'm giving Cali his bottle. We knew ahead of time that we would have to leave early today. We have to go to the Russian embassy to renew our visas again.

I say to Brian, "How can we leave now?"

"We don't have any choice," he says, "if we don't get the visa renewed today, we can't stay in the country. He's calm now, he'll sleep."

I finish feeding Cali and very carefully try to place him in his crib without waking him, but just as his body touches the mattress, his eyes pop open and he starts crying.

Zauri, who normally is the soul of patience, makes a grimace and taps on his watch to say we have to go. I put my thumb and index finger close together to beg one more minute. I lean over the crib and place my hand over Cali's tummy and make a slow circular motion. This often lulls him to sleep. Soon his eyes close.

As we leave the hospital, I gesture imploringly to the blond-haired woman in the front office to please check in on the baby. She nods yes, and I want to trust that she will, but I feel terribly uneasy leaving like this. The image of the string and the thought of the baby's unheard cries haunt me the long ride to the center of town.

*   *   *

We meet Olga at the Russian embassy and wait for an hour in a room filled with weary and discontented people. Olga is not able to explain to us, but it's evident that there is some problem with extending our visas.

We're taken into a small airless room. A bloated, blotchy-faced man is sitting behind a desk. We take a seat. Olga speaks with the man for a long while. He has the look and body language of a serious alcoholic, and appears to be giving Olga a difficult time.

Money seems to be the answer again. I'm not sure how much Olga has to dish out this time but again indicates to us that Natasha will pay. And again, this is not something we expected, but do deeply appreciate. Despite our problems in communication, Natasha has been more than honorable in her commitments.

We phone Eke as soon as we get home. "Besides the extension on our visas, was your mother able to make any further progress on finalizing the papers?" I ask. I tell her about the string and the fact that we could not find a nurse over the course of several hours.

"I will ask," Eke says.

There is some muffled talk in the background for several moments. Then Eke gets back on. "She says that she will not be able to do municipality until Thursday."

Today is Monday. "Why does she have to wait till Thursday?" I ask.

"I do not know," Eke says, wearily. She always sounds depressed over the phone. "She says we must also get signature from minister of justice."

"Minister of justice?" I say in disbelief. I look at Brian.

"What?" he says back in disgust.

I put down the receiver, and collapse on the armchair next to the phone. "That means possibly another week for the baby in the hospital," I say. "Another week before the papers can get to the American embassy, another week of insufficient care and attention . . . Where is the logic in all of this? They keep telling us that they want to finish this as soon as possible, that they want to keep this matter a "secret," and yet everything keeps getting delayed. All the hours, energy, and money—that have been wasted on this. And for what? So that a child can needlessly suffer?"

Brian tries calling Vaja but keeps getting a busy signal. After the tenth try, he says to me, "Go for a run in the park. It will make you feel better. I'm going to go to the post office and send a fax to Chairman Zhvania."

*   *   *

I run like a mad woman up the mountain. The threatening clouds mirror my own tempest. I welcome the heavy rain when it comes. I can cry out my agony, with no worry of anyone hearing or seeing me. I arrive home drenched but feeling somewhat better.

Tzira meets me at the door as I'm taking off my soggy sneakers. "Brian went to baby hospital."

"To baby hospital?" I say, looking up.

"He says, if he does not come back by ten, it means he is sleeping there."

"But how is he getting there?" I ask.

"He is taking minibus," Tzira says. "I give him number of bus and address of hospital so he can show driver."

A wave of guilt and worry rushes through me. Here I went for a run, and Brian's gone to the hospital. What if he gets lost? The hospital is far. How is he going to manage to get there at night without being able to speak a word of Georgian?

Era arrives with dinner.

"I'm sorry," I say to Tzira. "Could you tell Era I can't eat now?"

I can see from Era's face that she immediately understands.

"How can I help you?" Tzira asks me.

"I need to get to the hospital," I say. "I'm worried that Brian may not find it. Even if he does, I won't know because he won't be able to call me. The office is locked at night."

"You want Zauri to drive you?" she asks, knowing Zauri is waiting in the car for Era.

I nod.

*　　*　　*

We drop Era off at their apartment and continue on. Driving in silence with Zauri, I realize the hospital is even farther than I thought.

It's 10:00 p.m. when we arrive. I ring the bell several times. Finally, the door is opened by the tiny old woman who unlocked the bathroom door for me on that first day back in January. She smiles at me, and I'm reminded of her gold front tooth. Zauri says something to her and she shakes her head. It doesn't seem as though Brian is here. Zauri gestures to me to go look after the baby while he waits for Brian outside. I do not see a nurse on the floor. I walk swiftly down the long dim hallway to Cali's room. I find him with eyes wide open, staring at the ceiling. As soon as he sees me, he smiles broadly and puts out his arms for me to pick him up. I lift him out of the crib and hold him close. But where is Brian? An anxious half hour passes before he comes rushing in. He's surprised to see me.

"Thank God," I say, moving toward him. "Why didn't you tell me you were going to the hospital?"

"I didn't know how hard it would be to get here," he says. "I didn't want it to be dangerous for you." He puts his arms around me and the baby. We stand together in silence for several moments. Then Brian says, "It means so much to me that you came."

"Of course I would come," I say.

"I love you," he says.

"And I love you."

We stay with Cali until he falls asleep. He looks like an angel, his face all sweet and peaceful. Brian and I leave the hospital, deeper in our bond and commitment to each other, as well as to our son.

*   *   *

Dinner is still waiting for us when we get home. The homemade vodka is brought out. After the meal, Nia plays the flute for us. She plays skillfully and with such feeling. Then she and her mother sing some Georgian songs, and then we all sing American songs.

Tzira's ten-year-old grandson (from her other daughter, whose name is, of course, Eke) is sleeping over. When I ask Nia where the boy is going to sleep, she says, "With me. He loves to sleep in the bed with us."

Finally, we are let in on the sleeping situation. Nia tells us that she shares the bed with her mother and that her father sleeps next to them on a cot—four people in one tiny room.

Our street in Tbilisi

The Badridze family, our wonderful hosts.

On the way home we take a stroll through "Old Tbilisi."

With Nia, in the park on Victory Day.

Georgian boys singing and performing traditional Georgian Sword dance.

The Archbishop Elias II presides over the festivities.

Old-timers proudly display their World War II medals on Victory Day.

Many of the old-timers still cherish the memory of Georgian "Uncle Joe," and see him as the savior who delivered them from Hitler and the Nazis. The young people, and many, many others—strongly disagree.

The kind and generous Uberi family—a family of doctors. They did so much for us and never asked for anything in return. Behind are some of their uncle's paintings that survived the war in Abkhazia.

More Problems

May 13, 1997

Brian lets out a sigh as he puts down the receiver.

"What did Vaja say?" I ask.

"He says he tried to warn us about coming to Georgia before all the paperwork was completed. He says it's the agency's fault. He says they didn't give him the 'correct information' before the promise was made to Gilman."

"What information?" I ask.

"The information telling him and Chairman Zhvania the adoption would need to be approved by several ministries. He says we *do* need a signature from the minister of justice.

I look at Brian skeptically. "You would think Vaja would know what is involved."

"Apparently not," Brian says. "He says that the minister of education is frightened. He says Piradze has received appeals from many other families, and he mentioned again the one from Hillary Clinton."

"Why don't they just end the stupid moratorium?" I say, throwing up my arms in exasperation.

"Vaja says he just hopes our case is finalized before the 'new law' is passed, because that could complicate matters further."

*   *   *

Later in the afternoon on the grounds of the hospital, a young girl comes up to us as we're walking with Cali. He is nestled against my chest in the Bjorn bag.

"Why you take Georgian baby to America?" she asks in a hesitant English.

We're thrown for a second. Then I smile. She smiles back. Her manner is not unfriendly. I've seen her before. She is one of the refugees from Abkhazia living on the hospital grounds.

"We love him," I say.

She leans over and peeks at Cali, who is fast asleep. She looks back to us. "I want to go to America," she says, "but I have no money." She turns and points to the bombed-out hospital building where the refugees live. "I live there with my mother and father and brother. We have no house. Everything destroyed. My grandmother and uncle were killed in war. I want to study English, but I have no money for lessons."

I nod sympathetically, but I feel at a loss for what to say. What does one say to people who have been through war, who have lost everything? The thought flashes that I should at least offer to give a few English lessons while I'm here, but the young girl rushes off to join two other girls who are standing at a distance.

*   *   *

We stop at the American embassy to see Richard Thompson on our way back to the apartment. We tell him what's been happening. He says he's heard a 'rumor' that Georgian families are being allowed into the orphanage and are looking at the babies who have already been promised to American families.

"No!" I say, alarmed. "I thought Georgian families weren't adopting."

"Not your baby," he quickly reassures me.

It's wonderful if there are Georgian families who want to adopt, but not the same babies who have already been promised to other families.

*   *   *

May 14, 1997

We hear before leaving for the hospital that the minister of justice won't be back in town till Saturday. That means the first contact we can make with him is next Monday, at the earliest. Today is only Wednesday.

* * *

I bring Cali into Maly's room. I prop up a pillow in the little girl's crib and sit Cali against it. Maly is lying on her stomach. She's able to stand if she holds on to the bars, but strangely, she's not able to sit. She topples right over. She looks up occasionally at Cali, but mostly stares at me. There's a striking difference between the two babies now. Though Maly smiles easily, she seems, painfully, at the age of ten months, to have lost her innocence.

Cali's attention shifts between looking at Maly and looking at his fingers. At one point, when Maly moves closer to him, Cali reaches out and touches her hand lightly. He smiles. She stares back at him. I'm not sure if his smile is from touching the little girl's hand or from his own independent thoughts. It's a dreamy smile.

* * *

May 15, 1997

I've run out of paper this morning and have to write on this little memo pad. It's difficult to find regular notebook paper in Tbilisi.

One takes so many things for granted in the States. What we want—we go out and buy. Here, even with money, so many things are hard, or impossible, to find. Brian has been looking for shoelaces ever since he arrived. It's always a 'go and hunt for' situation. This little memo pad cost 250 lari. That's about $1.80. Not much for us, but how can the average person here afford this? I wonder what the students do. As Eke said back in January, they have wonderful universities, but no money for books.

Up till now, the level of education in Georgia has been very high. Literacy is over 90 percent. Will it continue this way, if the economic situation does not improve?

"I don't say that I would ever want Communism again," Tzira reflects, "but life was much easier then." She explains that her husband's salary was $250 a month, plus so many things were free—education, transportation, medical care, and cultural activities. "Now we have to pay for everything, and we have no money. That is why everyone must find many jobs."

What seems different in Georgia from many other poor countries I have visited is that people here are so well educated. Many seem overeducated and overqualified, as there is no outlet for their skills. Tzira tells us that the intellectuals and the well educated—doctors, scientists, teachers—are all poor.

Someone must have money here. There are a lot of Mercedes rolling around, as well as other fancy cars. Apparently, there's soon to be a concert by a famous Russian violinist. Tzira says it's sold out at $200 a ticket. Ray Charles was here last month. That concert was also sold out.

"There *are* rich people here," Tzira says, laughing. "Businessmen."

"What kind of businessmen?" Brian and I ask.

"I don't know," she says, raising her eyebrows and laughing even harder.

* * *

Michael phones us at 9:00 a.m. from our apartment in New York City. He says a lot of calls have been coming in expressing concern over our absence and situation. He wants to know if we have any idea when we'll be back. We tell him we don't know.

We haven't heard from Natasha in over a week. Has she given up on us? No, but her frustration is obvious. Dodo is still not back from London. Her three-day absence has turned into weeks. We so wish she were here. She seemed to have some 'in' with the ministers. Brian and I feebly joke that maybe Natasha has joined Dodo in London and they've opened up a Russian restaurant. We need to keep up our sense of humor. It's easy to get caught up in imaginings of what will happen if the minister of justice *doesn't* sign.

Era, our delightful, exuberant cook, is coming with us today to meet Cali. She's heard so many stories about him through Zauri and Tzira, and through our pantomimes.

On the way to the hospital, we stop at her apartment. She wants to take me upstairs and show me something. Brian and Zauri wait in the car.

Once again, I notice the enormous contrast between the devastation of the building and the warmth and care put into the personal living space. Era has me sit at a long antique wood table. She rushes to a large armoire and brings out a folder stuffed with photographs.

"Papa," she says, pointing to a picture of a man with a beard and what appears to be heavy makeup. "Singer . . . opera," Era says proudly. "Papa, big artist." She opens her arms wide to show me how big. And then bringing her hands together to allow for only a *small* space between, she says "Era" to let me know she considers herself a 'smaller artist.' She laughs, and says "baby" as explanation.

She and Zauri have two daughters who are in their early twenties. The older of the two has very serious diabetes. It began when she was four. She's losing her eyesight now.

"It is a tragedy," Tzira said the other night when we were talking about it. "But Era is always so gay. I don't know how I would be, in such situation."

I meet the daughter now. She's an outgoing young woman with a firm handshake and a deep voice. She's wearing dark glasses. I wouldn't know from seeing her how seriously sick she is, but Tzira says the doctors have not given much hope.

"Would you like something to eat or drink?" the young woman asks in English, as Era brings out a huge cake with a whipped topping. Era looks at her daughter with such love and pride.

"Oh, no, thank you," I say, holding my stomach. "I'm still full from the wonderful breakfast your mother brought this morning."

Era replaces the cake with what looks like a pudding. "Georgia," she says, meaning a specialty—and meaning something I cannot refuse. I take a couple of bites not wanting to offend. It's delicious. I can't help wondering, though, if the daughter is fed the intense sweets that Era is always offering us.

*　　*　　*

"Good baby, good baby," Era says, over and over again to me and to Cali, who is nestled in my arms. She loves it when he eats the porridge she prepared in the morning. It's easy to spoon-feed him now. So far, he's had sweet potato, carrots, egg yolk, applesauce, and porridge. He doesn't refuse anything and always screams for more with his strong voice. Speaking of which, Nia is taking us this afternoon to a student's competition in music, dance, and comedy.

*　　*　　*

Later, at Philharmonic Hall, the students are fantastic—a match for any performing arts school in New York. The first half involves students from the University of Tbilisi, and the second, students from the Music Conservatory. I'm particularly impressed with the students from the university. They are not even specializing in dance or music; nonetheless, they display enormous talent and skill.

"We learn the traditional songs and dances from time we are small children," Nia tells us.

At the beginning of each piece, whether it's harmonic singing, a classical piece on the piano, a Georgian mountain dance, an American jazz song, the audience immediately cheers, clearly recognizing the material.

I watch a particularly gifted young man play the violin and imagine Cali doing the same. I love it that Georgia has such a rich musical heritage.

*　　*　　*

May 16, 1997

Another hot day. Brian is hanging clothes on the line outside. We're so grateful to have this garden in back—for the beautiful red tulips that greet us every morning, and for a place to dry our clothes. We have to wash frequently as we brought very little clothing with us. Washing clothes and bathing are a challenge here with so little water trickling through the faucet. On the other hand, having our breakfast and dinner delivered and served to us seems an unnecessary luxury. So is Zauri's driving us to the hospital every day, now that we know how to get there on our own. But these services are a livelihood for them, and we don't want to deprive them of any potential income. Natasha continues to uphold her contractual agreement to cover our expenses—food, lodging, and transportation to and from the airport and hospital. She was thinking three or four days—*not four weeks*.

I also have the feeling Zauri and Era are helping simply because they want to. They are such kind, generous people. As are the Badridzes'. We've been made to feel a part of the family.

"I am so used to you," Tzira says to me when I go into the kitchen to get my tea, "that when you will leave, something will be missing."

It amazes me that in all the time we've been in Tbilisi, not a single person has tried to get us to slip them money under the table. We were warned to expect the opposite. It also amazes me that in this household, there has not been a single moment of discord. There are lively discussions, but no one ever raises a voice in anger. Nia absolutely adores her mother, and her mother adores her.

I think of how much my mother and I have missed in not having a closer connection.

*　　*　　*

We've just finished changing the baby's diapers and are about to feed him when Brian accidentally knocks over Cali's baby bottle, breaking it. There is not another spare bottle to be found in the entire hospital. Brian goes to see if he can find a baby bottle at the market that's about a mile down the road. Meanwhile, the doctor says we can *borrow* Maly's bottle.

I try speaking to the doctor about Maly. She is a new doctor on the floor and speaks a few words of English.

"She's very lonely," I say. "She cries all the time."

"She is *pretentious*," the doctor says.

The wrong use of the word is funny, but also sad. The inference is that if a baby cries and expresses her needs, she is not such a "good" baby.

*　　*　　*

May 17, 1997

The fortunate thing about the bottle breaking yesterday is that Brian bought a smaller bottle, which Cali is able to hold himself. He seems to delight in this control, but his smiles turn into a vale of tears when we make way to leave around five o'clock. He's never cried this intensely before. The nurses used to say "good baby" about him because he didn't cry so much. Maybe now he's "pretentious," too.

I take him in my arms and he immediately quiets. The moment I put him back in the crib, he starts wailing again. We send Zauri home on his own so we can stay with Cali until he calms down. It takes a long time to lull him to sleep.

*　　*　　*

From the hospital, we walk down the dusty road to the square that's about a mile away and wait for the bus. It's really more like a miniature van. Tzira calls it a "microbus." It costs 50 tetra for any distance, which is equivalent to about 35 cents.

We wait a long while, but it finally comes. The bus is packed and we have to squeeze in. I'm practically sitting on Brian's lap and he on the next person's lap. After about a half hour, the bus comes to a stop in the Old City. Everyone quickly gets out, and the driver signals to us that it's the end of the line. As we don't know how to ask which other bus to take, we decide to explore the Old City again and make our way home on foot.

We stop at Sioni Church. It's nice not to have to be a tourist this time. I take a seat on the bench off to the side. I close my eyes and surrender to the chanting and frankincense and glow from the candlelight.

I pray for the minister of justice to sign the papers without any more delay!

We find Rosteveli Avenue, but it soon begins to pour. We turn off onto a side street to look for shelter and come upon a strange sight—a modern, Western-style-looking hotel, with terraced cafe. The "Hotel Europa" it's called. We enter through huge glass doors. Large tropical plants frame an opulent lobby. We are welcomed by a black doorman in uniform (the first black person we've seen in Tbilisi). The cafe is full of people; the atmosphere very animated. It's an obviously affluent, international crowd. We hear snippets of conversations in German, French, Turkish, and English. It feels as though we could be in any large city in the world.

"Let's have a drink," Brian suggests.

It does us good to have a night out together, and worth the headache I get from the Cinzanos.

* * *

May 18, 1997

I'm walking down the hallway in the hospital on my way to the bathroom when I come upon a room I've never seen before. It's the 'color' that catches my eye through the slightly open door. I peek in. To my amazement, I see large red beach balls, a swing suspended from the ceiling, a playpen, mobiles, toys, etc. There are two nurses in the room, whom I don't recognize. They are standing over a baby who is lying on a table. They seem to be giving the baby a massage. One of the nurses catches sight of me. I smile and step back.

As I continue down the hallway to the bathroom, I wonder, how is it that we've never known about this room? I think of Cali's doctor telling us back in January that Cali *needed* massage. We had asked if it would be possible to get massage at the hospital and said we would cover the expense. When nothing was offered, we assumed nothing was available. And why would we not be told that there's a play area for children?

I pee and return to Cali's room. Brian has gone to the market to buy some diapers. Cali is lying on his back in the narrow crib, playing with his fingers. He looks up at me and stretches his arms out. I lift him up.

"Come on, little fella," I say, "we're going to go see something."

I take him to the *secret* room. I get looks from the two nurses. It's clear this room is not intended for us. Still, I put Cali into the playpen for a few minutes. I place one of the red beach balls beside him. He touches the ball lightly . . . then with a little more force. The ball rolls. A big smile spreads across Cali's face. I bring the ball back, and he pushes again. I look to the nurses. They smile self-consciously.

Dodo is Back!

May 19, 1997

Brian is on the phone when I come in from my run. "Dodo is back," he whispers, cupping his hand over the mouthpiece. "She says the minister of justice has signed and the municipality has been taken care of. She says we may be able to get Cali out of the hospital tomorrow afternoon."

I'm aware of suddenly feeling short of breath and light-headed. I grab hold of Brian's free arm. "Really?"

*   *   *

May 20, 1997

Dodo and Olga arrive early at the hospital. They meet us in the baby's room. Dodo doesn't mention her trip, and we don't ask, but it seems to have done her good. She seems more positive and energetic than when we saw her in January. She looks at Cali in my arms and smiles warmly. We assume she's here so we can take the baby out of the hospital, but our hope is soon dashed.

"There is teacher's strike," she says. "I was not able to get signature from municipality. I will try later."

She tinkles the baby's beetle socks and Cali laughs. I laugh with him, trying not to show my terrible disappointment. Dodo says how much happier and healthier Cali is looking. It has been a month since she has seen him. "He is completely changed baby," she says. I feel comfort in her words, but then tell her about the playroom I accidentally came upon and ask why Cali hasn't been allowed to go in there, especially since they had made such a point about his needing massage.

She sighs; then says, "I will ask."

I point to Maly through the glass window. She's crying in her crib, and there's no nurse attending to her. "She cries all the time," I say. "What is happening with the Greek people?"

Dodo sighs again. I can see she is genuinely concerned. We go into Maly's room. Dodo lifts the little girl into her arms. She sees the baby's blotchy face and hears her shallow breathing. "I will contact Greek embassy," she says, "but at this moment, you are only ones with permission to take out baby."

My joy at hearing Dodo say "permission to take out baby" is mixed with sadness. How can we take one child knowing so many others are left behind?

Dodo places Maly back in her crib. Maly immediately starts to cry.

"I will try to get her more food," Dodo says.

We both know food is not the solution.

*   *   *

Dodo returns in the afternoon and says that it does not look good for getting the baby out today, but she says we still may be able to leave for Moscow by tomorrow night. That seems overly optimistic considering the way things have gone so far. I ask her if she's spoken with Cali's doctor about the *secret room*.

"Yes," she says, hesitantly. "She says it is because baby had virus and massage would not have been good for him."

I suppose she's referring to the few days of diarrhea.

"But what about the play area?" I ask.

"It is probably for show," Dodo says, with a sigh of apology.

*   *   *

May 21, 1997

"I have good news," Tzira says as we come in from our evening hike in the hills. Nia, Nicholas, Zauri, and Era are gathered around Tzira as she greets us.

"Dodo says you must prepare your bags, as maybe you will be able to leave tomorrow."

"Did she get the municipality?" Brian asks.

"No," Tzira says, "but she thinks she will get it tomorrow."

"And what about the baby's passport and visa?" I ask.

"That she will get, too."

"And the American embassy?"

"Maybe," Tzira says. "Dodo is very energetic."

"And what about getting the baby out of the hospital?" I ask.

"That too," Tzira says, and laughs.

*   *   *

May 22, 1997

Zauri arrives at the hospital a little after 1:00 p.m. and waves a paper in front of us. We understand this to mean the hospital release.

"Dodo?" I say, thinking Dodo will come to help us take the baby out.

"No Dodo," Zauri says, and makes a sign that we are to leave now with the baby—and *fast*. He stands over us, urging us to hurry, as we dress Cali. We're assuming it's so that we can get home quickly to finish packing and make the plane that is leaving at five, but when we pass Cali's doctor on the way out and barely get a look our way, we suspect there must be *something* else.

I almost feel as though we're kidnapping Cali, which, by this point, would be fine with me. The refugee girl we met the other day comes up to us as we step out of the hospital. She's with the same friend. She has an instamatic camera and wants her friend to take a picture of her with the baby and me.

"How do they know?" I whisper to Brian.

"Nothing like secrets for the word to get out," he whispers back.

I look to Zauri to see if we have time to stop. He shrugs, and then nods. We have our camera, too, and I make a sign to the girls that I would like to take a photo of the two of them with Cali. This seems to please them very much. I take several shots. The girls speak to Zauri, and he replies. He must be telling them that we're leaving, I think. The refugee girl immediately advances to hug Cali and me. "I love you very much," she says.

She and her friend walk with us to the car. As we're getting in, she says, "I wish you big success in America and happy life."

Cali and I are in the backseat. I suddenly feel overcome with emotion, but do my best to restrain my tears. I roll the window down further.

"We wish you a happy life, too," I say.

She is a very pretty young girl, with bright eyes, full of warmth and longing.

*   *   *

We arrive at the Badridzes. It's surprising how Cali immediately accepts his new environment. He doesn't seem at all afraid of the new space or the new faces. He observes everything with a kind of serene calm.

Tzira says it is amazing that Cali looks so much like me.

"Maybe I was Georgian in another life," I say, smiling at Cali.

Nicholas says something now to Tzira and points to Cali's left hand.

"He says baby reaches with left hand more than with right," Tzira tells us. "He thinks baby will be left-handed."

"Maybe he has the makings of a baseball pitcher," Brian says.

"How about an artist?" I counter. "Did you know a large percentage of the world's greatest artists and geniuses have been left-handed?"

* * *

Dodo phones at 2:30 p.m. to say she will pick us up at 3:00 p.m. to drive us to the airport. Nia holds Cali while we make a mad scramble to finish packing our suitcases.

Ten minutes later, the phone rings again.

"Dodo says it is not possible to leave today," Nia tells us. "She says American embassy needs more time for papers."

We don't understand.

"Is Dodo only now taking our papers to the embassy?" I ask.

Nia nods.

Brian calls the American embassy. He speaks with Richard Thompson, who reports that he has not seen Dodo, or our documents.

"How is that possible?" I ask.

"But he says," Brian goes on, "that if Dodo can get the papers to him in the next half hour, he will check to see if everything is in order, and we might still be able to leave tonight."

We try calling Dodo at home. Her mother answers. We hand the phone to Tzira.

"She says that Dodo has gone to change your plane tickets," Tzira explains.

Why didn't she finish with the American embassy before getting us tickets to Moscow? Brian and I wonder.

Soon, Era arrives with dinner. Tzira asks Era if she has heard anything further about Dodo. Era replies at length. Finally, Tzira turns to us and says, "Dodo has gone to a wake."

A wake? We don't know whether to laugh or cry.

Now we may not be able to leave until next Wednesday. The American embassy in Moscow is closed on Saturday and then it's Memorial Day on Monday.

Torrential rains break loose at dusk. Who knows, maybe we are being protected.

Nicholas assembles a crib from some old pieces of wood that were in the shed. I put Cali in the crib for a short while, but when we go to bed, I place him on my mattress on the floor to sleep between us.

* * *

May 23, 1997

Eke arrives at 10:00 a.m. She tells us that Dodo is waiting in the car.

"You must come, too." There's urgency in her voice. She looks at Cali who is in my arms. "With baby," she says. "We must go to orphanage."

"Orphanage?" I say, feeling a sharp pain in my chest. "What for?"

"I don't know," Eke says, her face taking on its look of strain. "They say you were not supposed to leave hospital without hospital's permission."

"I'm not taking the baby back to the orphanage," I say. "Not over my dead body."

"Just relax," Brian says. "Nothing is going to happen."

"It is just to show them you are the parents," Eke says.

"They can't take the baby?" I cry, wanting to make a statement, but hearing a question come out instead.

"No," Eke says. "Baby has passport."

"So why go?" I persist.

"You must go," she says, starting to get impatient with me.

"I'm not going."

"You cannot leave Georgia with baby until they give you release."

"We'd better go," Brian says.

I look to him. How can he say that?

"We're not going to leave you ever again," I keep whispering to Cali, as the huge padlock on the iron-gate is unlocked and we enter the orphanage—a foreboding looking, brick building.

There is much commotion going on in the dimly lit, narrow entranceway, as women in white coats rush past us to enter and exit rooms to the right and to the left of us. I had expected to see a room packed with many cribs, but we do not see, or hear, any children. It feels eerie.

We are led into a large office. It is a bright, sunny room with a couch to one side, a table, and some chairs.

"This is chief doctor's office," Dodo says, motioning us to take a seat on the couch that is against the wall.

Three women in white come in while we are waiting for the chief. They smile at us, make a passing glance at Cali, speak with Dodo, and then leave.

The chief enters now. He is a big man, with a huge gut and bulging fish eyes. He doesn't even look at Cali. I'm glad. I find him repulsive.

He and Dodo immediately get into a heated discussion. We are not included in the conversation. I can see that Dodo is trying to be both ingratiating and persuasive. This continues for at least an hour. Then Dodo tells us that they want a *signed* statement that will explain who we are, where we come from, and that we have adopted this baby. This seems an absurd request as the Georgian government has a very extensive dossier on us, including our home study, with all kinds of personal information. I'm worried and suspicious, but we don't have much choice.

"Yes, of course," we say.

Brian writes a short paragraph giving the information, preceded by "with the kind assistance and permission of President Shevardnadze and Chairman Zhvania . . ."

*　　*　　*

"The problem is because of Mrs. Shevardnadze," Dodo explains when we are all safely in the car. "She and her women's group are against foreign adoption. She was in orphanage a few days ago, and she told chief that if he hears of your baby going from hospital to let her know at once."

"Who would tell her from the hospital?" I ask. "The chief doctor there? She did act very strange when we left. She seemed angry."

"She was not angry," Dodo says. "She was afraid."

*　　*　　*

We drive straight to the American embassy and bring Cali inside with us. We present all our documents to Richard Thompson.

He smiles at the baby, but then says, "We'll need a release from the orphanage."

"A release?" Brian says. "But we just barely managed to get out of there."

"I understand it's a problem," Thompson says, "but it's not a frivolous thing. I could let it pass, but I don't want you to have trouble at the American embassy in Moscow. See what you can do and I'll use whatever influence I can."

We go back to the car. Dodo is visibly upset. "Why they ask for this?" she says. "They never ask before. Baby was most time in hospital. We have 'release' from hospital. American embassy always tries to make it difficult for us. I swear to you over body of my daughter, that yesterday, Thompson said to me it was *impossible* to do papers immediately. He was absolute."

It's true. I could see there was a definite difference in the way Thompson related to Eke and Dodo, and the way he treated us.

"I will see what I can do," Dodo says, dropping us off at the house.

"Let's get a breath of fresh air," I suggest to Brian.

We take Cali to Victory Park. In spite of our troubles, it is exciting to go on our first family outing in *freedom*.

The cable car is working today. Walking toward it, I say, "let's give the baby a view of Tbilisi."

What a joy to share with Cali the thrill of arriving at the mountaintop. He seems to love the vibrant colors all around him—the chorus of birds, the sweet, cool air; and mostly, having the two of us continually dote on him.

*   *   *

When we return, there is a call from the American embassy.

"You are free to leave Georgia," Thompson's assistant tells us enthusiastically. "The embassy in Moscow has waived the release from the orphanage."

Oh, please, let it be true this time! We have reservations to leave for Moscow on Monday.

*   *   *

May 25, 1997

We decide to take advantage of our last remaining weekend to see more of the Georgian countryside. Zauri wants to take us to Manglisi, a small mountain village, known for its ideal altitude and climate for children with respiratory problems. Cali still has a little cough.

It's a gorgeous drive, but extremely bumpy. Cali is agitated. His first tooth is coming in. I sit in the backseat with him, trying to cushion the blows. Zauri does what he can to dodge the potholes, but between the car's poor suspension and the torn-up dirt road, it's rough.

Cali calms down as soon as we get out of the car in Manglisi. Brian carries him in the Bjorn bag. We see bands of little piglets and ducklings, calves, and lambs wandering with their mamas though the dirt streets of the village. Groups of small children stop to stare at us.

We continue walking into the hills behind the village. It's beautiful and lush. The air smells delicious. I'm reminded of Switzerland, with the verdant mountains, the dazzling array of wildflowers, the babbling brooks—everything looks so alive and pure.

We come upon an ancient-looking woman, all wrinkles and bones, sitting alone on the grass. She's leaning against a stick, one leg propped up at the knee, the other leg straight out. She has a kerchief around her head and a tattered apron over a flowered dress. She seems to have her eyes closed. We try to pass without disturbing her, but suddenly, she opens her eyes and sees us. She quickly pulls her dress down over her exposed knee. We nod to her. She nods back. She sees that we're carrying a baby. She stands up. I'm amazed at her spryness. We stop in front of her. Holding on to her stick, she leans toward the baby. Cali looks to her, squinting in the sunlight. The old woman smiles back, revealing a toothless mouth and twinkling eyes. It's an almost mystical moment—the exchange between old crone and infant child.

*   *   *

In the evening, Dodo calls. She says that she had a "big argument" with Mrs. Shevardnadze's group of women.

"I had to tell them that you left the country already."

*   *   *

May 26, 1997

We're leaving today for Moscow. Our Memorial Day and, fittingly, it also happens to be Georgian Independence Day.

Tzira places a small pear-shaped clay frieze in my hand. "A keepsake," she says. "A Georgian castle." Then she gives me a tape of Hamlet Gonashvilli, one of Georgia's most beloved singers. "It is not a new tape, but I think it will still be good."

This family has been so incredibly generous with us. I will miss them all very much—especially Tzira. I will always remember her kindness and her words, "How can I help you?"

"You have shown me what being a mother is all about," I say to her.

She smiles and hugs me; and then hugs Brian. Then Nia and Nicholas open their arms to embrace us.

Dodo arrives. She says she cannot accompany us to the airport. "I must say goodbye here," she says. "Vaja says to me it may not be safe. He says Mrs. Shevardnadze's group could try to 'stop us.' They will recognize me, but do not know what you look like."

She tells us that the chief of the orphanage was fired at the orders of Mrs. Shevardnadze. "But it is good thing," Dodo says. "He was a bad man." She also hugs us warmly and gives Cali a kiss. "I know he will be very happy with you."

Zauri also does not drive us. A young blond-haired man we've never seen before is our driver. Eke is the one familiar face. She comes along to translate.

We look over our shoulders the entire ride to the airport, trying to spot someone following us. Eke is not allowed inside the turn-style, and we are on our own. We struggle with our bags, holding Cali in one hand and our documents in the other. We try to appear nonchalant as we show our passports to the customs officer. He takes his time looking at our papers, looking at us, looking at Cali. At long last, he stamps our passports and nods that we can continue. Our hearts are still pounding as we line up outside the tiny plane, waiting to go up the ramp. Not until the plane taxis off the runway and leaves the ground do we exhale a long awaited sigh of relief. I've never felt so safe to be on an airplane.

"We're on our way home, Cali!"

*   *   *

Cali, "all dressed up and ready to go."

The refugee girls say goodbye.

And a sad goodbye to our friend. We worry who will feed him when
we are gone.

Brian with Zauri and Era

Our first weekend out, Zauri takes us for a ride to the in the country.

On our hike, we meet an old Georgian peasant woman. It was like something out of a fairytale.

Moscow

May 26, 1997

"Voucher, voucher," the customs woman in Moscow repeats to us.

We don't know what voucher means. Her supervisor comes over.

"We need to see voucher for your hotel," the supervisor says.

We know not to say that we are *not* staying in a hotel, but we are not quite sure what to say.

"You have tourist visa," the supervisor says.

"We're being sponsored by the U.S. Congress," Brian says as he pulls out the baby's adoption papers and the letter to Shevardnadze.

This does not seem to impress the young supervisor.

"Sit, sit," he says to me several times, pointing to Cali in my arms. "Is heavy."

I remain standing.

"No problem, no problem," he says to Brian, and then in the next breath says, "Big problem."

We tell him that this is what the Russian embassy in Tbilisi issued us.

"Please, speak to our Russian coordinator," I say. "She is waiting here to pick us up."

Ten minutes later, Nadya arrives. "How could they do this?" she says, referring to the visa, an edge of hysteria in her voice. "You will have to go back to Georgia."

"What?" we say. She must see the panic in our faces.

"Wait," she says, "I will try."

She huddles privately with the supervisor and pleads on behalf of the child. Finally, the supervisor allows us to enter, but warns that we may run into trouble when we try to leave Moscow.

*   *   *

May 27, 1997

We stay the night in a private apartment and have the whole place to ourselves. Though it is in a tenement building, we enjoy luxuries we didn't have in Georgia—a bath with hot water.

The improved economic situation here is visible even in Moscow's dogs. In the park nearby, we see beautiful, well-fed dogs of all pedigrees. I miss the strays at the hospital in Tbilisi. They were starting to trust and depend on us.

Nadya's exactitude is a bit trying after the laid-back manner in Georgia, but it serves us well. She gets us to the Russian doctor promptly at 8:00 a.m. for Cali's medical examination for U.S. Immigration. Cali is pronounced 'healthy,' and we are quickly whisked off to the American embassy. We are in the door by 9:00 a.m. We are the fourth family to arrive, and, within an hour, the place is packed. I am amazed at the number of Russian children being adopted, children of all ages. Nadya tells us that these are the numbers every day.

We are able to leave by 11:00 a.m. and told to return at 5:00 p.m. to pick up the visa and the sealed envelope containing Cali's medical report.

Nadya gets us back to the embassy right on time. Names are called out one after the other. There is clapping with each name. I can feel my heart racing.

"Hickey," the young black woman behind the desk suddenly calls out. I feel a gasp inside.

"Congratulations," she says, smiling. She extends a large brown envelope to us.

I know all the days have been building up to this moment, but still the 'shock' is unexpected. I feel an explosion of emotion, with a cascade of tears and laughter. It's definite now! No ifs, ands, or buts. This is the confirmation. Cali is ours!

*   *   *

May 28, 1997

We breeze through customs and are aboard the plane. Cali is all smiles and totally alert as we take off. He seems to like flying. It wasn't really intentional, but decked out in his new baseball jacket and cap Cali is wearing red, white, and blue.

Two adorable little Russian girls sitting across the aisle come pay us a visit. They are sisters, aged four and five, also just adopted. It's so sweet to see them be affectionate with Cali, and it's the first time he's really relating of his own, not simply reacting.

I have never felt so happy, so exultant!

*   *   *

2007

Cali is now ten. He's tall, handsome, smart, outgoing, funny, creative, and the love of our lives. I'm not saying that there haven't been challenges. There have been. But so far, there has been nothing that love, truth, patience, and acceptance have not made better. We know there is a long road ahead, and that there will be more challenges, different challenges. Hopefully, we will meet these with courage and understanding.

It's hard for me to believe, looking back, that when I first began this journey I wondered whether I could be a mother. There was so much fear and self-doubt. Fortunately, there was another voice inside urging me on.

I see now how destiny propelled me on this journey, with all its unknowns, obstacles, and wrenching concerns, so that I would really *know* that I *wanted* this child, that I would fight for him and love him. Nearly every adoptive parent I've spoken with feels a very deep sense that they have found the *perfect* child for them, that somehow they and their child were destined to be together. I know this is true for me, and I know that through Cali I have discovered a depth of love I didn't know I was even capable of feeling.

When we left the hospital in May 1997, Maly was still in her crib, her face grotesquely contorted, her screams for attention heartbreaking. The Greek couple never did get her. The moratorium prevented that. Eventually, she was adopted by a Georgian family. If only she hadn't had to wait so long and endure so much pain.

How many Malys throughout the world still wait?

*　　*　　*

Safe at home on our deck in Garrison.

Cali having breakfast with the boys, Myshkin and Frenchie.

The three of us a few years ago at the Cape.

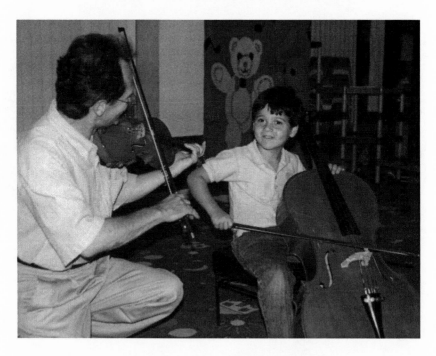

Cali with his music teacher, Dr. Lehman

Cali does a sword dance of his own, decked out in his Georgian hat and vest, gifts from Dodo.

Cali and I on the beach in France.

Cali today.

Postscript

My story should not in any way be construed as a criticism of adoption agencies, or even of our agency. I have told my story as I experienced it, in the heat and passion of the moment. In retrospect, I came to realize, as the reader can no doubt see, that we had been warned, we just didn't really hear it, or want to hear it. We were preoccupied with our baby—and solely focused upon his welfare. Our agency was concerned with all the babies, and doing what they could to protect their access. In the end, they behaved honorably and far exceeded their contractual obligations to us.

Similarly, my story should not be taken as a condemnation of the Georgian government, or, a trivialization of the complicated issues involved in international adoption. Without the kindness and empathy of many Georgians, in and out of the government, our adoption could not have taken place. In any case, the Georgian government of 1997 no longer exists. It was removed from power by the peaceful, populist Rose Revolution of 2003.

*　　*　　*

Acknowledgements

I embarked upon this path long after the death of my father. And though references to him are sparse, his presence in my heart is a constant. Cali carries his name, the name of his grandfather—Odon. I know my father would have loved Cali. They would have played ball, gone fishing together, and have been great friends.

As my father's generosity helped make all of this possible, so has my husband's love and commitment. Brian has accompanied me every step of the way on this journey. Without him, I never could have done it.

*　*　*

There are many people who helped bring this book into being.

My deepest gratitude to Sylvia Perera who first encouraged me to make a committed project of this; and for her faith, wisdom, and nurturing support.

To the late Bill Longgood for his uncompromising honesty, and generosity of spirit.

Thanks to Suzanne McConnell for her inspiring writing class, where I first began this as a short story.

Many thanks to Gay Walley for her enthusiastic guidance and keen "writer's eye,"

Appreciation for the editorial assistance of Irene Glazios and Penny Franklin.

Warmest thanks to the many friends who were part of this adventure. Ed Setrakian, Rena Foreman, Belinda Wolmack, Viviane Lind, Didi Conn, Peter Reznik, Catherine Shainberg, the late Shelly Winters, Barbara Zinn,

Joe Lynch, my New School students, Lee Hickey, Michael Hickey and Susan Stemont, the Badridze family, Zauri and Era, the Uberi family, and, of course, Dodo.

A note of special appreciation to David Soumbadze for his sensitivity and understanding.

An eternal debt of gratitude to Congressman Benjamin Gilman.

*   *   *

Lastly, I want to thank my mother. As I have grown as a mother, I have also grown in understanding and compassion for her. I recognize that she, too, was a child, had a mother, and had a history. My mother gave me what she could, and what she could not give me, she tried to provide through others. In both joy and pain, I thank her for providing the experiences that led me on the road to Cali.

References

Karen, Robert. Becoming Attached: *First Relationships and How They Shape Our Capacity to Love,* Oxford University Press, Inc. Re-released 1998

Encyclopaedia Britannica: Macropedia
Fifteen Edition: Volume 28. 1995

How Much is That Doggie in the Window
Words and Music by Bob Merrill.1952

Cover photos by Corinne Chateau and Brian Hickey. All other photos by Corinne Chateau and Brian Hickey, or from their personal collection. Page 166, in Old Tblisii taken by Maka Uberi. Page 197 in Garrison, taken by Clelment Skalski, Page 198, Cape Cod, anonymous, and page 200, bottom, 2007 school photo.